ENTERTAINING

ENTERTAINING

MALCOLM HILLIER

DK

DORLING KINDERSLEY

LONDON · NEW YORK
SYDNEY · MOSCOW

A DORLING KINDERSLEY BOOK

Visit us on the World Wide Web at
http://www.dk.com

PROJECT EDITOR Lesley Malkin
DESIGNER Murdo Culver
ASSISTANT DESIGNER Pauline Clarke
DTP DESIGNER Robert Campbell
PRODUCTION CONTROLLER Hélène Lamassoure
SENIOR MANAGING EDITOR Mary-Clare Jerram
MANAGING ART EDITOR Amanda Lunn

PHOTOGRAPHY Stephen Hayward
FOOD PHOTOGRAPHY Martin Brigdale
STYLIST Helen Trent
FOOD STYLISTS Janice Murfitt, Jane Suthering

First published in Great Britain in 1997
by Dorling Kindersley Limited
9 Henrietta Street, London WC2E 8PS

ISBN 07513 04565

Text film output by R&B Creative Services,
Great Britain

Reproduced by Colourpath
Printed and bound in Great Britain by
Butler and Tanner Ltd, Frome and London

CONTENTS

RECIPE SYMBOL GUIDE

PREPARATION TIME   COOKING TIME
OTHER TIME REQUIRED

HOSTING A

"Never eat more than you can lift" MISS PIGGY, A PUPPET

THE FIRST STEP
I love the planning almost as much as the event: it is certainly all part of the fun that entertaining at home is supposed to be.

WHEN I WAS STILL STUDYING MUSIC, I became captivated by the idea of entertaining. To create a special time at home when people could appreciate each others' company and share some delicious food seemed the most exciting of prospects. A great friend and I used to vie with each other, as impoverished students, to produce the least expensive but most glamorous meal. Times have changed, but we have never looked back.

A lunch for two, a supper for six, a dinner for twelve, or a buffet party for a crowd: I still think little beats the pleasure of entertaining a group of friends or family, enjoying food, drink, and lively conversation in your own home. Such events become milestones to anticipate, and then remember.

We all want the occasions on which we entertain to be a success. Although some effort is required to orchestrate any event so it proceeds smoothly with a minimum of worry, I find this effort is almost always richly rewarded. Remember also, that the simplest of meals is frequently just as enjoyable as a more elaborate spread.

PARTY

Kitchen entertaining is what I enjoy most. Fortunately, my country kitchen in the centre of London, with a large window overlooking the garden, is capacious enough for a table that will seat ten, leaving plenty of cooking space. The formal dining room down the hallway has been made into an office. I no longer feel isolated from guests while I prepare the food, and I believe my guests are much more relaxed about the whole dining experience, too.

Entertaining can be one of the great joys of life; it is one of mine. I have close friends who give an informal dinner party in their kitchen, every week, often for as many as twelve people. They say that it keeps them young, and to prove it they are still doing it in their mid-eighties. So send out the invitations, and prepare for you and your guests to enjoy yourselves.

DECIDING ON THE OCCASION

EXOTIC EVENING

All these dishes are subtly, yet interestingly, spiced to give a well-balanced exotic menu. *Serves 6*

PEPPERED SCALLOPS
Two colourful sauces accompany the peppery scallops.

LAMB TAGINE WITH COUSCOUS
Tender young lamb stuffed with a piquant-sweet mix of spices, herbs, and prunes.

COCONUT & SAFFRON ICE CREAM
A dreamy, creamy concoction with flavours and textures that are irresistible.

DRINKS
An oaked, buttery New World Chardonnay with the scallops, and a full, rich, spicy Australian Shiraz with the tagine, is ideal. Serve a chilled sweet white port with the ice cream.

PLANNING NOTES
The ice cream can be made up to six weeks ahead. Prepare the stuffing for the lamb tagine in advance, if necessary. The two sauces for the scallops can be prepared ahead of time, kept covered with clingfilm in the refrigerator, then heated through for serving. See pages 86–7 for recipes.

IDEAL PARTNERS
Always make sure that the food you serve suits the occasion and looks impressive with the table decorations you choose.

WHETHER THE DECISION TO ENTERTAIN springs from a simple desire to have a party, or you have some friends you would like to see, planning an event, in my mind, is as important as the event itself.

If it begins with the guests, how best to entertain them? Would they prefer a lazy lunch, an elegant dinner, a summer barbecue, or a refined tea? On the other hand, if your motivation is the occasion itself, you will need to decide on a guest list to suit the event. I always try to assemble a group that has at least one linking thread of interest, and invite a good conversationalist. Also consider any restraints: how much time and expense can you spare? How much room (including oven and refrigerator space) do you have, and are you confident in catering for and entertaining large numbers?

TAKING CARE OF THE DETAILS

I find a party is easier to orchestrate if I plan it around a theme, perhaps dictated by the food I serve or the season: a vegetarian winter supper, an Italian buffet, or a summer barbecue. Plan the table setting and food presentation, remembering that small touches make all the difference.

COUNTRY HAMPER
PICNIC

FESTIVE CELEBRATION
DINNER

CHAMPAGNE
BUFFET

Entertaining is the very stuff of life

Inviting your guests can usually be done informally over the telephone: this often means an instant reply, and gives you the opportunity to enquire about food dislikes or allergies. If you wish, send written invitations to make it more of an event. Remember to include a dress code, particularly if your theme requires it, as well as the reason for the party if it is a celebration.

WHAT FOOD TO SERVE

The key to a successful menu is balance: choose interesting ingredients, and consider how their flavours, colours, and textures interact with one another. Bear in mind that the freshest ingredients in season are always best. It is simple to mix and match the recipes given here, referring to the planning notes on each menu, as long as you always remember no two courses should be too rich. Never take on too much; it is vital that you are relaxed and at ease while you cook and entertain. Your guests will sense if you are not.

CONSIDER YOUR DRINKS

The type of occasion and the food you plan to serve are important considerations when deciding what to drink with your meal: a refined wine and fiery barbecue food will not do justice to each other. Serving an aperitif before the meal is a great way to relax your friends, but do make sure it is not so strong that it spoils the first course. A brandy, liqueur, or port with coffee after the meal is also welcome, especially in winter. When calculating how much wine to buy, I usually allow, on average, three glasses per person with the meal. Always stock up on mineral water and one other soft drink.

CROCKERY CHOICE

PLATE STYLES
Creamware is ideal for regular use, while elegant white with marbled edging suits more formal occasions. If you want a change buy some inexpensive coloured plates.

MOST OF US HAVE ONLY ONE whole set of china backed up by a motley collection of unmatching plates, bowls, and dishes for everyday eating. If you entertain a great deal, the ideal situation is to have two whole sets, each with twelve settings. One is for everyday use, and should include tea- and breakfastware. This set can be used for informal entertaining. The second could be a grander, more special affair for formal occasions.

BUYING NEW CROCKERY

Starting afresh with new tableware is both exciting and daunting. The choice available is enormous, so it is important to reflect on what might affect your final decision. Firstly, consider your lifestyle: there is little point in buying expensive and delicate china when you usually eat informally around the kitchen table; similarly, if you prefer to entertain in style, chunky plates in bright colours may not be that appropriate. Today, buying dishwasher-proof tableware puts little design restriction on choice, and is a distinct advantage. Take note of the shapes and sizes of the plates in a given range. Soup bowls should always be a good size, and I believe main plates are comfortable at about 25cm (10in) in diameter. Larger than this, they are awkward to wash and store;

smaller, and the plate can look overcrowded. I find that flat dessert plates are often much more useful than bowls, and side plates should be large enough to serve salad on. Salad bowls are best in wood and pottery. Three covered serving dishes, a large carving plate, and two sauce boats are important extras.

THE FOOD ON THE PLATE

As the appearance of food varies enormously, there is much to be said for choosing very plain china. For everyday, a stylish all-white or cream plate with some interesting moulding, such as fluting or scalloped edges, is hard to better; most food looks attractive against white. Plates of all one colour, particularly yellow, green, and pale blue, also set off food well. Rich, bright colours can look splendid with some dishes, but horrendous with others. Choose them as inexpensive, light-hearted alternatives to more versatile but perhaps less exciting crockery, to ring the changes.

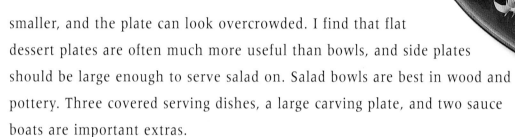

IMPROVISE WITH WHAT YOU HAVE

Almost all china can look good on an attractively set out table. To make the most of what you already own, echo the colours in it, in lighter or darker shades, elsewhere on the table. Do not be afraid to mix and match plates of a

similar style if you do not have enough of one design: use the napkins, flowers, or candles to provide a link.

Look beyond your usual crockery to find alternative vessels, and introduce unusual elements to reinforce a theme:

a large sea shell for salt on a nautical table, or a hand-crafted ice bowl from which to serve sorbet or ice cream. Presentation is very important, and it is amazing how you can create a completely new look with what you already have.

FOOD PRESENTATION
When you are deciding on which plates to serve each course, consider how to display the colours and textures of the served food to best advantage.

WHICH GLASS?

GLASSES ARE AVAILABLE for every type of drink from champagne to cider, from Rully to Friuli, from bitter to stout, from Cloudy Bay to Beyond My Wildest Dreams, and from piña colada to tequila sunrise. You would need an enormous range of glassware to satisfy your thirsty guests in precisely the right glass, so I recommend you choose just a few types to cover the drinks most usually served. For before the meal, you may need a set of champagne flutes; tall tumblers such as a Collins glass for soft drinks, water, long mixed drinks, and beer; low tumblers for whiskey; and sherry glasses. During the meal, large-bowled red wine glasses, good-sized incurving white wine glasses, and water glasses will suffice. Afterwards, you may need brandy glasses, port glasses, and liqueur glasses. All others are luxuries. I like clear, colourless glasses best, particularly for serving wine, but there is an ever-widening selection of most attractive coloured glasses available for when you would like a change of scene.

WHAT TO SERVE WHEN

For before a meal, I usually make up a jug of one drink, such as Pimms, rum punch, or vodka and cranberry juice. This simplifies serving, particularly if you are greeting new arrivals at the same time, and you can always provide a one-off for anyone who may not like your choice. Always offer a soft alternative such as fruit punch.

On special occasions, it is a great treat to serve more than one wine with the meal; this is not necessary for informal meals. Have a plentiful supply of mineral water, too. Finish off by serving a brandy, port, or liqueur with coffee, perhaps away from the table to help structure the event. When entertaining casually, stemmed multi-purpose glasses can be used for most pre-meal drinks, red or white wine, and water.

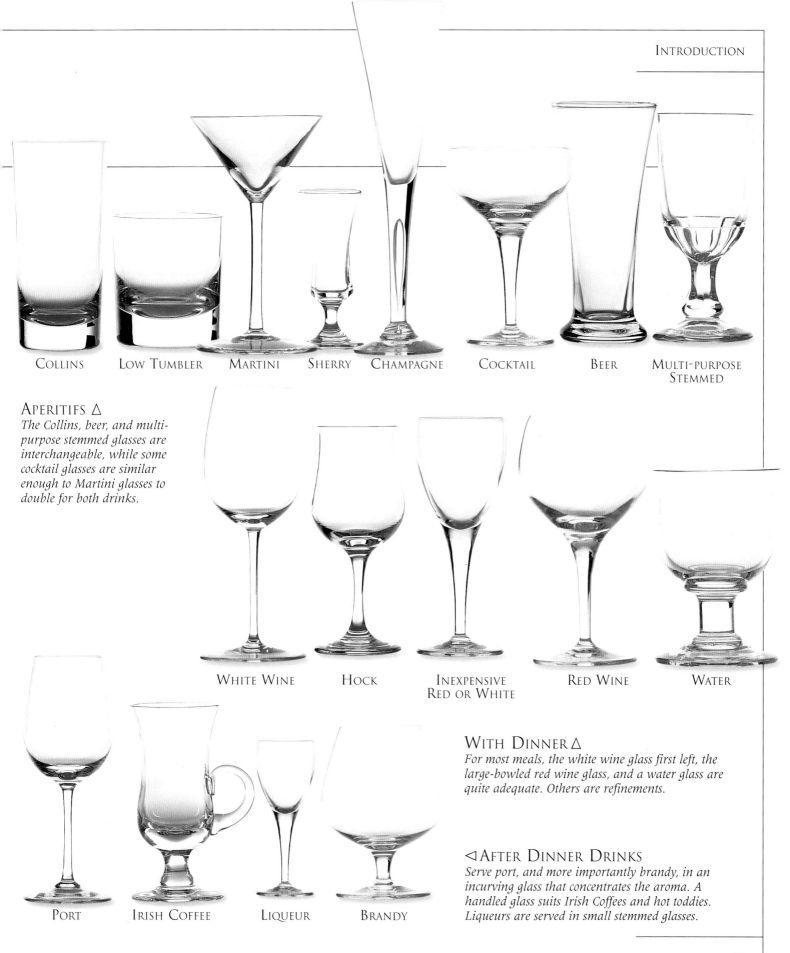

COLLINS LOW TUMBLER MARTINI SHERRY CHAMPAGNE COCKTAIL BEER MULTI-PURPOSE STEMMED

WHITE WINE HOCK INEXPENSIVE RED OR WHITE RED WINE WATER

PORT IRISH COFFEE LIQUEUR BRANDY

APERITIFS △
The Collins, beer, and multi-purpose stemmed glasses are interchangeable, while some cocktail glasses are similar enough to Martini glasses to double for both drinks.

WITH DINNER △
For most meals, the white wine glass first left, the large-bowled red wine glass, and a water glass are quite adequate. Others are refinements.

◁ AFTER DINNER DRINKS
Serve port, and more importantly brandy, in an incurving glass that concentrates the aroma. A handled glass suits Irish Coffees and hot toddies. Liqueurs are served in small stemmed glasses.

FLOWERS TO IMPRESS · A daisy is

THE PRESENCE OF FLOWERS lends a grace to any and every occasion. Choose your flowers carefully, then take the time to condition them to ensure they look at their best for your party. A few basic items of equipment are essential. For informal displays, you will need a good pair of florists' scissors, a pair of secateurs for cutting woody stems, a small, sharp knife for scraping stems, and buckets in which to condition flowers (use jugs or vases for smaller flowers). For more complex arrangements, you may need florists' foam, chicken wire, stub wires, wire cutters, florists' gum, and prongs.

ARRANGING FLOWERS
Do this well ahead, leaving you time to perfect the food.

SCHEDULE
Buy flowers about three days in advance, condition them, and store in buckets until you are ready to arrange them.

FLOWER CHOICE

First decide on the type of arrangement (or arrangements) you want at your party. Where would you like to display it? How much space is available? What vases or other receptacles do you have? What flowers are in season? Do they tie in with, or can they dictate, your colour scheme? Low displays are most suitable for the table, but larger bold ones can really impress; either have one on the dining table until guests sit down to eat, or place on a side table or mantlepiece. Gain inspiration from the gallery on the right, which

INDIVIDUAL TREATMENT

All flowers and foliage should be conditioned as described opposite, but certain plant types need additional special treatment. The hard stems of woody shrubs must be cut at an angle as usual, then the base of each stem hammered to a pulp, so it takes up water more efficiently. Scrape 5cm (2in) of the bark as usual.

Milky-sapped plants, such as euphorbia and poppy, need to be seared in a flame once cut to stop them weeping. Cut flowers may have been seared by the florist already.

Some plants, most notably tulips, Corsican hellebore, and privet, are so acidic they adversely affect other flowers, so are best displayed alone.

every bit as beautiful as an orchid

shows the range of displays in the book, for ideas for table, individual place setting, side table, wall, and mantlepiece arrangements.

CONDITIONING

I usually buy flowers three days in advance of the occasion, selecting specimens that are just beyond the bud stage, with healthy fresh leaves. Check stems that have been underwater have little or no paling and are clean of slimy bacteria.

When you return home, prepare all plant material by cutting the ends of the stems at a sharp angle, and scraping 5cm (2in) around each stem up from the base. Remove any leaves that will be submerged in the final arrangement, and plunge the flowers or foliage into a bucket of water with three or four drops of household bleach added (this inhibits the bacteria that causes plants to rot). Leave in a cool, light (not sunny) place for at least two hours, but preferably overnight or until buds have opened and you do the arrangement, ideally the day before the event. Keep the buckets outside when it is cool to prolong plant material's life.

Once arranged, change the water regularly, adding a few drops of bleach each time. Drooping stems can sometimes be revived by placing their ends into boiling water for five to ten minutes.

FLOWER GALLERY

pages 66–7

pages 30–1

page 64

pages 49–51

pages 72–3

pages 108–9

pages 46–7

pages 126–27

page 142

page 141

pages 110–11

page 157

page 33

page 170

pages 172–73

LIGHTING

THE NATURE AND LEVEL of lighting plays a key role in creating the right atmosphere for your entertainment: it can definitely make or break an occasion. During the day you have less control, though inside, blinds are effective for shading intrusive rays of sun through windows, and on gloomy days candlelight can be most welcome. Outside, for the sake of both guests and the food, the area where you sit and eat should be shaded. Some of my most memorable meals have been enjoyed outside in the soft dappled shade of a vine canopy.

CANDLE EFFECT

In the evening, candles give a soft and flattering light that creates an easy ambience in which people seem to flourish. Candlelight alone may not be sufficient to serve and eat by, so add a little gentle electric illumination to make sure the level of brightness feels just right.

As well as using candlesticks and candelabras, consider including candles in floral displays, or make lanterns. Outside, candles need to be protected from a breeze. Though glass candle protectors are readily available, you can improvise your own by placing candles in drinking glasses. Remember that scented candles, such as rosemary, citronella, and lemon, are excellent at keeping insects at bay.

TABLE DISPLAYS

pages 72–3   *pages 124–25*   *pages 140–41*

pages 68–9   *page 69*   *page 107*

CANDLE SAFETY

Never leave candles burning unattended. Inside, in particular, light candles only when someone can keep an eye on them. Position them carefully out of the way of individuals serving food, where they will not impede the view across the table, or scorch flower arrangements or walls.

Candles used in displays with fresh flowers are moderately safe, as the plant material is unlikely to catch fire and the container has water in it. Do ensure, however, that the candles are always taller than or well away from flowers and leaves.

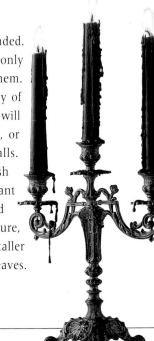

TABLE LINEN

THE MOST INVITING dinner tables I have seen often owe much of their appeal to the table linen: the cloth and the napkins. Consider the colour of the cloth carefully as it dominates the look of the table; I believe in keeping it plain. If you are buying new table linen, neutral colours are the most useful; white, cream, and pale grey are all favourites of mine, but of the darker colours, holly green and rich dark red can look magnificent, especially in winter. Wooden table surfaces are soft and mellow, but it is most important to use place mats to prevent scratches and heat damage to the table. Choose them to co-ordinate with the table decorations and napkins.

THE DETAILS

Much old-fashioned formality has now disappeared, but I am always disappointed if I do not have a crisply laundered plain or damask linen napkin in a restaurant. Cloth napkins engender a great sense of luxury at home, too, and although they may involve more work afterwards, their contribution to the overall effect makes them well worth the effort for the majority of occasions. For large parties, paper napkins are more practical, though. I prefer a simple rolled or folded napkin, maybe with a decorative ring or tie.

NAPKIN IDEAS

pages 28–31

pages 156–57

pages 64–5

pages 32–3

pages 46–7

pages 48–9

pages 172–73

pages 142–43

pages 140–41

NAPKIN RINGS

Use plaited raffia or ribbon, wire-edged for best effect, to make your own napkin rings. It is very simple, and is a most effective way of linking the assorted decorative elements of your table together.

THE PLACE SETTING Fortunately,

A NAGGING, BUT UNNECESSARY, CONCERN often surrounds the order in which cutlery should be placed when laying a dining table. The simple convention (below) is that knives, forks, and spoons are placed in course order, from the outside inwards, on either side of a central plate. A knife for bread is placed on the extreme right. Water and wine glasses stand on the right above the knives, and the side plate with its napkin sits on the left beyond the cutlery. As an alternative, the napkin could be placed on the central plate, and the bread knife on the side plate. All this would be reversed for a left-handed guest. If this layout takes up too much space around your table, consider the more informal options (right).

FORMAL SETTING
This setting is for four courses: soup, then a savoury first course, followed by the main course, and a dessert. Two wines will be served. A charger plate adds to the formality of the setting.

SIDE PLATE
Placed to the left of the main plate, this often has the napkin on it, and is used for bread or salad.

CHARGER PLATE
A optional large decorative plate remains in place throughout the meal.

eating peas off a knife is not easy

WINE GLASSES
The glass used first, usually for white wine, is set closest to the plate.

WATER GLASS
Place this above the knives.

CUTLERY
Arrange in the order of the courses, from the outside in, with extras such as the bread knife on the outside.

ALTERNATIVE LAYOUT

Table settings can easily be adapted from the conventional one (left) for less formal occasions and to limit the amount of lateral space occupied by each place; perhaps when entertaining more than six people around the average-sized dining table. Two possible alternatives are shown below.

INFORMAL SETTING
Here, the dessert spoon and fork are laid above the plate, spoon above fork, with the handles pointing in the direction in which they will be picked up. Place the napkin on the central plate or side plate.

MINIMALIST
Unless the first course and the main course are too divergent in flavour, use the same knife and fork for both. A cutlery rest helps to keep the table clean. Use an informal wine glass for wine and/or water.

LAYING A DINING TABLE

WHEN LAYING A TABLE, your main concern should be the comfort of your guests, and the ease with which they can converse with one another. Ideally, I like each individual to be able to talk to everyone present. With more than eight people, this can become difficult, unless you have an oval table. As my dining table is rectangular, the ideal number of guests seems to be six: it gives unity to the group and appears to prevent anyone from feeling isolated. With a larger number seated at a rectangular table, the group often polarizes into two; on such occasions, I ask some guests to swap places between courses.

Some hosts resent missing out on conversation while cooking during the meal, and so prefer to entertain in the kitchen. This also means hot food stays that way between oven and table, but it is an arrangement that may not suit less confident cooks. Bear in mind that the accumulation of debris as the occasion progresses can be unsightly!

SPACE FOR COMFORT

The dining table must never feel crowded. Where space is limited, serve away from the table rather than trying to fit serving bowls in the centre. Condiments, bread, and salad should be easily accessible: for more than six people have two cruet sets on the table.

An arrangement of flowers, however simple, always makes the table feel well dressed and, certainly for evening meals, the glow of candles adds to the atmosphere. Ensure they do not occupy too much space or obstruct guests' vision lines. I often have a large arrangement on the table until guests sit down, when I move it to a side table for the meal. Small vases at each place are attractive and less intrusive.

▽ THE WELL-DRESSED TABLE
The dining table should never feel intimidating, even for the grandest of dinners. In every aspect of its decoration, make the comfort of your guests the absolute top priority.

SALT AND PEPPER
Allow one cruet set per six people; small bowls of salt crystals and coarse pepper are a good alternative.

DINING ERGONOMICS

To enable guests to cut their food and use a fork with ease, allow about 65cm (26in) between the centre of each place setting. Leave enough room in the middle of the table for essential condiments. Aim to achieve a balance between enabling your guests to help themselves to items so you are not continually attending to their needs, but strive to keep the table uncluttered. If you have flowers and candles on the table, make sure people can see one another clearly over them.

SALAD BOWL
Space now occupied by the salad bowl held an impressive floral display before guests were seated.

FLOWERS
Small, well-balanced vases or bowls hold individual flower arrangements.

WATER JUG
A jug of bottled or tap water on the table allows guests to help themselves.

LAYING A BUFFET TABLE

AS BUFFETS GENERALLY CATER for large numbers of guests, easy access is the main requirement of a well-laid table. Where possible, have two serving stations (one food, one drink), and make food that is simple to eat and serve.

For a self-service buffet, a table that guests can walk around is ideal, but in many homes space restrictions mean the table will be against a wall, and the queue will feed along one side of it, as shown below. Lay items out in the order they are to be collected: the plates, cutlery, and napkins first, followed by the main dishes; any dressings, condiments, bread, and salad

SELF-SERVICE ON ONE SIDE
This buffet of two pasta dishes with salad, is set out for guests to help themselves along the front of a table against a wall.

ESSENTIAL TOOLS
Arrange cutlery so that it is easy to pick up.

NAPKINS
Provide sufficient paper napkins for each guest to use more than one.

PASTA BOWLS
Serving dishes for hot food should not be too large; replenish them frequently.

SALAD
For a buffet, choose small salad leaves that are easy to eat.

SALT AND PEPPER
Guests can take pinches of coarse pepper and sea salt: spoons easily tip over small bowls.

should be close by. To save having to lay dessert plates and cutlery out during the meal, place them further down the table away from the savoury courses. Site any low flower and candle decorations in inaccessible spaces at the back, or between the items needed for one course and the next. Red wine, or white wine in a cooler, can be judiciously placed for refills, away from the main flow for food.

BREAD AND BUTTER
Cut both bread and butter into manageable-sized pieces.

FLOWERS
Position a low bowl of flowers where it will not obstruct serving.

DESSERT ITEMS
Bowls, spoons, and ratafias await the arrival of ice cream.

CATERING FOR A CROWD

The tables below are set for large numbers. An all-round setting allows more guests to help themselves to food at a time than does the table against a wall (see left). For more than 18, it is worth stationing someone behind the table to serve the main dishes.

ALL-ROUND ACCESS
As for all buffet settings, lay the plates, cutlery, and napkins first. Place main dishes next, with extras such as Parmesan cheese and condiments close at hand. Salad, bread, butter, extra salt and pepper, and drinks with glasses (laid on the table as there is room) follow round to complete the circuit.

SERVER BEHIND THE TABLE
The main dishes (at the back of the table) are served by a host or waiter, but guests help themselves to cutlery, napkins, salad, bread, butter, and condiments (all situated at the front of the table). There is space for wine, but not glasses. Ensure that hot food replenishments can arrive without disruption.

COUNTDOWN TO THE EVENT

FIRST DRINKS
Set out drinks and glasses in readiness for pouring as soon as your guests arrive.

SHOPPING
Plan to shop more than once: this allows you to purchase items that were unavailable or that you may have forgotten to buy first time around.

THE KEY TO KEEPING CALM is having everything well ordered: you will feel much more at ease and, consequently, so will your guests. Making lists may sound dull but, when organizing an event, I cannot do without them.

DECISIONS, LISTS, AND SCHEDULES

Once you have chosen a menu and settled on a theme, make a shopping list of all the ingredients needed, including drinks to be ordered, remembering non-alcoholic drinks, and tea and coffee. Decide on flowers or other special items like candles that you may require and add these to your shopping list. Next, plan a detailed cooking schedule, always including early preparation tasks such as marinating.

Now is the time to consider the format of the actual occasion itself. Plan exactly where each stage of the event should take place, from pre-meal drinks to coffee afterwards. When this is decided, make a second schedule of non-cooking tasks, such as arranging flowers, preparing any special items, laying the table, tidying up, and drawing up a seating plan. Include on this list reminders of tasks to be done during the event too, such as adjusting the central heating, preheating the oven, or removing sorbet from the freezer to soften. Closer to the event, it may help to combine your cooking and non-cooking schedules.

"Perfection is the child

THE TIME APPROACHES

While cooking, I frequently find a second timer is a useful reminder of non-cooking tasks that still need to be completed. Try, if you can, to leave plenty of time for any hitches, as well as a restorative tea or coffee break. Strike out the jobs on your lists as you complete them: this is both satisfying and reassuring.

Make sure each space you will be using is tidy and welcoming, and set up what you need in each room before everyone arrives: lay a drinks tray in readiness and place cups and saucers where you plan to serve coffee. Decide on a division of tasks if more than one of you is hosting the event.

LAST-MINUTE PANIC

Do remember to allow time to get yourself ready. There is bound to be some last-minute cooking, however much you prepare in advance, but a few minutes of relaxation with a drink before the door bell rings is a lifesaver.

of time" JOSEPH HALL 1574–1656

SCHEDULE

▷ **SEVERAL WEEKS BEFORE**
Decide to have a party
Consider who to invite
Issue invitations
Choose a menu
Hire any help or equipment that you may need

▷ **THE WEEK BEFORE**
Prepare food, drink, and flowers shopping list
Write out party schedule
Cook food that can be frozen
Decide rooms in which you will entertain

▷ **THREE DAYS BEFORE**
Buy and condition flowers
Make relevant table decorations
Buy drinks

▷ **THE PREVIOUS DAY**
Shop for food
Arrange flowers
Tidy up and iron table linen
Make sure you have a good supply of ice
Prepare food that can be kept overnight

▷ **THE DAY OF THE PARTY**
Prepare as much food in advance as possible
Do all cooking that can be reheated
    at the last minute
Prepare rooms where you will be entertaining
Set out drinks tray
Bring wines to correct temperatures

▷ **A FEW HOURS BEFORE**
Lay table
Decide on seating plan
Start any early cooking

▷ **THE LAST HOUR**
Have as much cooking as possible underway
Tidy kitchen; wash up
Get ready yourself
Open red wines to breathe
Have a stiff drink – you deserve it!

▷ **AT THE PARTY**
For lunch or dinner parties, allow 1¼ hours
from the first guest arriving to starting the meal

BREAKFAST & BRUNCH

THE FIRST MEAL OF THE DAY
IS A PARTICULAR AND SPECIAL
ONE, AWAKENING APPETITES ANEW.
SERVED AS A HEARTY FAMILY FEAST, A
SPREAD FOR A SELECT GATHERING OF FRIENDS,
OR AN INTIMATE REPAST FOR TWO, IT SHOULD ALWAYS BE
HOMELY, RELAXED, AND INFORMAL. THE DISHES ARE ONES OF WHICH
WE NEVER TIRE: I SO RELISH THE TASTE-PACKED MIX OF THESE SIMPLE FOODS
THAT I AM OFTEN TEMPTED TO PREPARE THEM FOR LUNCH AND DINNER, TOO!

*A rustic setting outdoors (right) provides the perfect context for the delicious
flavours of the Late Summer Brunch menu (page 34).*

RUSTIC

A brilliant morning, and the air is buzzing

CREATE A RUSTIC Provençal atmosphere in which to enjoy a late breakfast or even later brunch, with golden tableware set on a sky-blue plank table.

LINING A BASKET

Use a good-sized napkin or tea cloth to line a basket for your breakfast rolls, toast, or chunks of bread. This flower-like liner will keep bread deliciously warm.

SKY-BLUE TABLE
This plank table is painted with a blue wash. If you have an old wooden table, paint on one coat to complement your tableware.

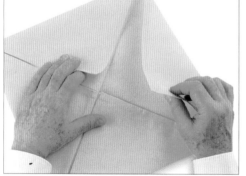

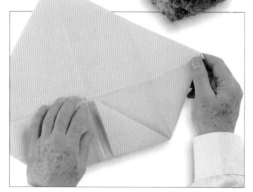

1 Spread a large square napkin or tea cloth, right side facing down, on a table or other flat surface. Fold each of the four corners to meet exactly in the centre.

2 Preserving the folds you have made, carefully turn the napkin over and fold each corner to meet exactly in the centre once again.

3 Place in the basket, holding down the ends in the centre. Bring each loose corner up from underneath, making a flowery nest for your bread rolls.

Find the loose corners and bring them over

28

with promise

SLAB OF BUTTER
A chunk of farm-fresh butter on a pottery dish needs no fussy arranging; its uneven form makes it tempting.

BREAD BASKET
Wicker has an easy informality that is suited to most day-time eating; add a flower-folded napkin to keep the bread warm.

RAFFIA TIES
Choose plain napkins that tone in with the colour of your crockery. Secure each one with a plaited raffia tie (page 31).

EVOKE SUNSHINE IN THE DETAILS

MORNING FLOWERS

Simple flower arrangements are most appropriate
for a relaxed breakfast or brunch. Every season
offers a range of plant material, particularly if
you select flowers, leaves, and berries for
their textures as well as their colours.
The colour scheme of these two
summer displays is drawn from
the warm sunny shades of the
crockery on page 28. If at all
possible, choose flowers that
complement your own tableware.

Butterfly Weed

MARIGOLD BASKET
*Some flower species, such
as these marigolds, offer a range
of shades in the same colour
band. A yellow basket, lined to
make it waterproof, shows them
off most attractively.*

COLOUR HARMONY
*Rich orange provides an
important foil to the bright
yellow, lime green, and red
of the other plants.*

The secret is natural rustic simplicity

Dill

Marigold

St John's Wort

Miniature Sunflower

WEATHERED CONTAINER
This old watering can makes an exciting rustic container. I have lined it with a plastic bucket to ensure it stays watertight.

NAPKIN FANS

Neutral-coloured napkin ties made from plaited raffia will suit any rustic daytime feast. I have teamed them here with sunny yellow linen napkins, but all weights of cotton will work well.

1 Fold one third of a square linen napkin in and smooth down. Make small even concertina folds at right angles to the initial fold to form a fan; you can iron these in.

2 Divide about 30 strands of raffia, 35cm (14in) in length, into three, and plait. Secure each end with a single strand and knot the tie around the bulky end of the napkin fan.

INDULGENT

Breakfast together, companions for ever

FOR A LUXURIANT and intimate breakfast in bed, set trays in advance, have the brioche ready to warm, champagne chilled, and the coffee pot waiting.

LOVER'S ROSE HEART

Ensure a romantic start to the day by making a simple, sweet-scented heart to grace the breakfast tray. Moss frames the flowers, and galax leaves adorn the sides.

1 Wrap the base and sides of a piece of soaked florists' foam in plastic. Trim the plastic to fit, and secure with adhesive tape.

2 Cut one side of each galax leaf straight, to align with the base of the foam. Apply glue along the straight edge.

3 Glue each leaf to the side of the heart. Pin the unglued top part to the foam, but do not pierce the base or it will leak.

4 Overlap the leaves all the way round to completely cover the sides. Trim the rose stems to 2.5cm (1in) each, and stick in the centre of the foam shape. Tuck a ruff of Spanish moss between the leaves and roses to finish the heart.

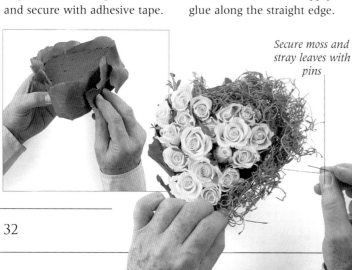

Secure moss and stray leaves with pins

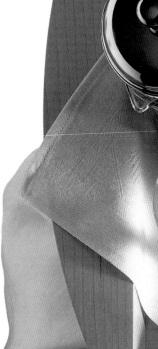

ROSE IN A NAPKIN
Fold a large linen napkin into a triangle then wrap it around a single rose.

LINEN TRAY CLOTH
As a tray cloth, use a linen napkin that matches the one holding the rose.

LEMON CURD
Decant an individual portion of home-made lemon curd into a small bowl for the tray.

MENUS

Good food in the morning makes the rest

WHOLESOME START

Impress a small crowd, or just a few close friends, with this colourful cosmopolitan menu. *Serves 6*

MANGO & PAPAYA
A bright fan of exotic fruits with a squeeze of lime.

PROVENÇAL PIPÉRADE
An easy-to-make French omelette, encapsulating flavours of the Mediterranean.

CRANBERRY MUFFINS
Delicious muffins, as American as the Stars and Stripes.

DRINKS
A large jug of cranberry juice to start, and an invigorating rosehip or hibiscus tisane to accompany the meal.

PLANNING NOTES
Make the muffins and lightly cook the pipérade vegetables the day before. Early on the day, slice the mango and papaya, squeezing the lime juice over them to prevent discolouration. Pipérade is best eaten fresh, so assemble it during the meal, using two pans if you are making more than six portions. *See pages 36–7 for recipes.*

LATE SUMMER BRUNCH

The tantalizing flavours and colours of this alfresco country feast are just reward for the time spent preparing it. *Serves 12*

PERNOD PEARS IN GRAPEFRUIT JUICE
The piquant juice is perfect with pears.

PROSCIUTTO, PRAWNS & APPLES
Best enjoyed freshly made; a delicious combination.

GOLDEN CORN & GREEN PEA PANCAKES
Tasty by themselves, these pancakes are a good base for the prosciutto, prawns, and apples.

DRINKS
One part Campari to six parts ruby orange juice makes a refreshing start. Offer hot Arabica coffee throughout the meal.

PLANNING NOTES
Prepare the Pernod pears a day ahead to allow the flavours to develop. Pancakes freeze well, so you can make them several days in advance; defrost the night before, and reheat in a hot oven before serving. Cook the prosciutto, prawns, and apples just before serving, after making or reheating the pancakes. *See pages 38–9 for recipes.*

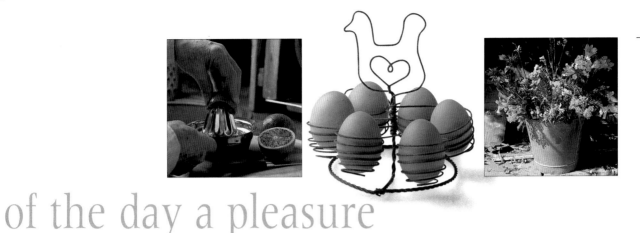

of the day a pleasure

LOVERS' BREAKFAST

Indulge in the exciting colours, spicy tastes, and interesting textures of this exotic breakfast menu.
Serves 2

COEUR À LA CRÈME & PASSION FRUIT
Make a romantic start to the day with heart-shaped moulds of curd cheese and yogurt.

SPICY KEDGEREE
A successful mix of smoked fish and spicy rice.

RICH LEMON CURD
Creamy lemon curd tastes wonderful on a light-textured bread such as brioche.

DRINKS
Mix two-thirds Champagne and one-third freshly squeezed orange juice to celebrate the new day. End with strong Arabica coffee.

PLANNING NOTES
Lemon curd can be made well in advance and lasts for up to three months in the refrigerator. The coeur à la crème must be made the day before to allow it to drip overnight. Prepare the kedgeree the day before; simply heat it through in a moderate oven for 12 minutes just before serving, while you are squeezing the oranges to go with the champagne.
See pages 40–1 for recipes.

WINTER BREAKFAST

The traditional hearty British breakfast is one of those great meals. Serve this refined version at weekends as a leisurely treat for special guests.
Serves 6

BUBBLE & SQUEAK
Coarsely crushed potatoes and cabbage, with bacon, baked crisp and golden.

HERBED TOMATOES
Tomato halves, baked with sprigs of wild herbs.

CREAMY SCRAMBLED EGGS
Delicious comfort food, best served immediately after cooking.

TOAST WITH ORANGE & LIME MARMALADE
Lightly toasted wholemeal bread complements this typically British preserve.

DRINKS
A large cafetiere of Kenya coffee, refreshed frequently.

PLANNING NOTES
Prepare the bubble and squeak ingredients the day before, but do not bake. On the day, bake the bubble and squeak, and chop the herbs for the tomatoes. Bake the tomatoes and make the scrambled egg while the bubble and squeak is cooking, immediately before eating. *See pages 42–3 for recipes.*

WHOLESOME START FOR 6

MANGO & PAPAYA

15 MINUTES

INGREDIENTS
3 LARGE RIPE MANGOES
2 LARGE RIPE PAPAYA
2 LIMES, JUICE ONLY
CASTER SUGAR TO TASTE (OPTIONAL)
MINT SPRIGS TO GARNISH

1 Peel the mangoes with a potato peeler and cut each one into 6 slices, slicing lengthways, parallel to the flat side of the stone.

2 Peel the papaya, cut in half lengthways, then scoop out and discard the seeds. Cut each piece of fruit into 9 slices across the width of each half.

3 Arrange 3 slices of mango and 3 slices of papaya on each plate in a fan shape and drizzle lime juice over each serving. For a sweeter salad, sprinkle a little caster sugar over the top. Garnish with a sprig of mint.

COOK'S TIP
Pineapple, kiwi fruit, or banana can be used in addition to, or instead of, the mango and papaya. This delicious dish also makes a simple and refreshing dessert.

PROVENÇAL
PIPÉRADE

PROVENÇAL PIPÉRADE

 10 MINUTES 20 MINUTES

INGREDIENTS

3 TBSP OLIVE OIL

175G (6OZ) SMOKED HAM, CUT INTO 2.5CM (1IN) STRIPS

4 SHALLOTS, THINLY SLICED

1 RED PEPPER, THINLY SLICED

1 GARLIC CLOVE, CRUSHED

2 TSP FRESH THYME (PREFERABLY LEMON THYME), FINELY CHOPPED

3 PLUM TOMATOES, SKINNED & CHOPPED

175G (6OZ) NEW POTATOES, SCRUBBED, COOKED, & DICED

SALT & PEPPER TO TASTE

30G (1OZ) BUTTER

12 EGGS, LIGHTLY BEATEN

1 Heat 1 tablespoon of the oil in a frying pan. Add the ham and cook for about 2 minutes on each side, until just brown. Transfer to a warmed dish to keep hot in the oven.

2 To the pan, add the shallots, red pepper, garlic, and thyme and cook over a moderate heat for about 10 minutes, until just softened.

3 Add the tomatoes and potatoes and continue to cook for about 15 minutes, until all of the liquid has been absorbed. Adjust seasoning.

4 Heat the remaining oil and the butter in a large frying pan. Pour in the eggs and stir until softly scrambled. Remove the pan from the heat and spoon the vegetable mixture over the eggs. Finally, top with the warm ham and sprinkle with coarse ground black pepper. Serve immediately with lightly buttered toast.

COOK'S TIP

The vegetable mixture can be prepared a day in advance and just warmed gently in a saucepan. The ham and eggs, however, should be cooked immediately before serving.

CRANBERRY MUFFINS

 20 MINUTES 20 MINUTES

INGREDIENTS

75G (2½ OZ) PORRIDGE OATS

200ML (7FL OZ) MILK, WARMED

8 TBSP PLAIN FLOUR

½ TSP BICARBONATE OF SODA

1½ TSP BAKING POWDER

PINCH OF SALT

1 LARGE EGG, LIGHTLY BEATEN

6 TBSP LIGHT SOFT BROWN SUGAR

30G (1OZ) BUTTER, MELTED

90G (3OZ) CRANBERRIES OR 60G (2OZ) BLUEBERRIES, COARSELY CHOPPED

1 Preheat oven to 200°C/400°F/Gas 6. Place the oats in a large mixing bowl and pour over the milk. Stir well and set aside for approximately 10–15 minutes to cool.

2 Meanwhile, in another mixing bowl, sift together the flour, bicarbonate of soda, baking powder, and salt. Add the egg and sugar to the oatmeal mixture, and beat well. Stir in the sifted ingredients, alternating with the butter and cranberries.

3 Divide the mixture between 12 x 7.5cm (3in) muffin tins, or strong paper muffin cases. Bake for about 18–20 minutes, until golden. Leave the muffins in their tins for about 5 minutes, then turn them out onto a wire rack. Serve warm with unsalted butter.

COOK'S TIP

For sweeter muffins, use the fresh blueberries instead of cranberries.

CRANBERRY MUFFINS

LATE SUMMER BRUNCH FOR 12

PERNOD PEARS IN GRAPEFRUIT JUICE

— 20 MINUTES   30 MINUTES —

INGREDIENTS

12 PEARS, NOT QUITE RIPE
1 LITRE (1¾ PT) PINK GRAPEFRUIT JUICE
90G (3OZ) CASTER SUGAR
12 STAR ANISE
175ML (6FL OZ) ANISEED LIQUEUR
(PREFERABLY PERNOD)

1 Halve, peel, and core the pears. Place in a large saucepan, pour over the grapefruit juice, and add the sugar and star anise.

2 Bring to the boil, cover, and simmer for about 15–20 minutes, until the pears are just tender.

3 Transfer the pears to a serving dish. Boil down the juice left in the pan until it has reduced by about half.

4 Strain the juice into a jug and allow to cool. Add the Pernod. Pour the liquid over the pears and refrigerate until ready to serve.

COOK'S TIPS

These pears can be prepared the day before they are required. For a non-alcoholic alternative to Pernod try ginger ale, or ginger cordial, omitting the sugar from the recipe.

PROSCIUTTO, PRAWNS & APPLES

— 10 MINUTES   20 MINUTES —

INGREDIENTS

6 CRISP RED EATING APPLES (PREFERABLY JONAGOLD)
½ LEMON, JUICE ONLY
2½ TBSP SUGAR
500G (1LB) RAW TIGER PRAWNS
3 TBSP VEGETABLE OIL
10 SPRIGS EACH OF FRESH
THYME & MARJORAM
SALT & PEPPER TO TASTE
500G (1LB) PROSCIUTTO, VERY THINLY SLICED
4 TBSP OLIVE OIL
250G (8OZ) MIXED MUSHROOMS, SLICED

1 Preheat oven to the lowest setting. Cut each apple into 12 slices and remove the core. Place the slices in a bowl and sprinkle with the lemon juice and sugar. Prepare the prawns (see Step 1, page 94).

2 Heat the vegetable oil in a large frying pan and fry the apples with the herbs for about 5 minutes, until golden. Season lightly. Transfer to a warmed dish to keep hot in the oven.

3 Fry the prosciutto slices in the pan for about 5 minutes, until crisp, turning frequently. Place on a baking sheet and keep warm in the oven.

4 In the same pan, heat the olive oil and sauté the mushrooms for about 5 minutes. Remove with a slotted spoon and place with the prosciutto slices in the oven.

5 In the same oil, sauté the tiger prawns for about 2 minutes, until they turn pink. Transfer everything to a large serving dish and and serve with Golden Corn & Green Pea Pancakes (see opposite).

COOK'S TIP

The cooking times for the apples and mushrooms will vary according to the varieties used. They both need to be *al dente* and not overcooked.

GOLDEN CORN & GREEN PEA PANCAKES

10 MINUTES · 35 MINUTES · 30 MINUTES CHILLING

INGREDIENTS
175G (6OZ) PLAIN FLOUR, SIFTED
175G (6OZ) CORNMEAL, SIFTED
275G (9OZ) BUTTER
900ML (1½ PT) MILK
6 EGGS, LIGHTLY BEATEN
350G (12OZ) FROZEN CORN KERNELS, THAWED
250G (8OZ) FROZEN PETIT POIS, THAWED
3 TBSP EACH FRESH PARSLEY &
CHIVES, COARSELY CHOPPED
1½ TBSP FRESH THYME, FINELY CHOPPED
SALT & PEPPER TO TASTE
GREEN SALAD LEAVES & CRÈME FRAÎCHE
TO SERVE

1 In a large bowl, mix the flour and cornmeal. Heat 200g (7oz) of the butter to melting point.

2 Gradually whisk the milk, eggs, and melted butter into the flour mixture. Stir in the corn, peas, herbs, and seasoning. Cover and refrigerate for at least 30 minutes. Stir.

3 Place 2 teaspoons of the remaining butter into a 25cm (10in) frying pan and heat until the butter just browns.

4 Put 2 tablespoons of batter into the pan. Cook for approximately 1 minute on each side, until golden. Transfer to a wire rack in the oven to keep warm, and repeat with the remaining batter.

5 Place the pancakes on a bed of green salad leaves and serve with Prosciutto, Prawns & Apples (see opposite) and a dollop of crème fraîche, or with bacon and maple syrup.

COOK'S TIP
These pancakes can be cooked a day in advance. To warm again for serving, arrange on 2 or 3 large baking sheets, wrap the sheets loosely with foil, and reheat in a moderate oven for about 15 minutes.

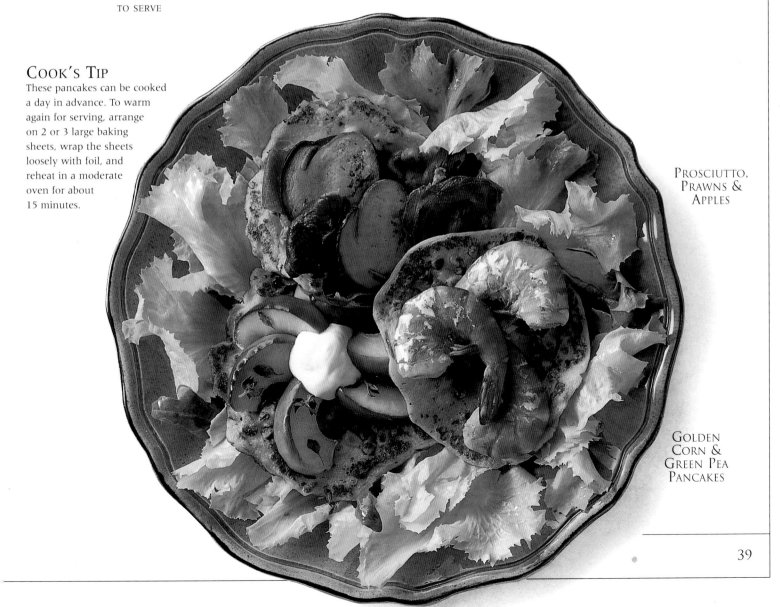

PROSCIUTTO, PRAWNS & APPLES

GOLDEN CORN & GREEN PEA PANCAKES

LOVERS' BREAKFAST FOR 2

COEUR À LA CRÈME & PASSION FRUIT

☑ 15 MINUTES ☐ 12 HOURS COOLING

INGREDIENTS
6 TBSP CURD CHEESE
4 TBSP LOW-FAT FROMAGE FRAIS
6 TBSP LOW-FAT GREEK YOGURT
1 TBSP CASTER SUGAR
1 TSP VANILLA EXTRACT
1 LARGE EGG, WHITE ONLY
2 PASSION FRUITS
1 TBSP ICING SUGAR, SIFTED
SOFT FRUITS TO DECORATE

COOK'S TIP
A raspberry or strawberry coulis makes a delicious alternative to passion fruit.

1 Beat together the curd cheese, fromage frais, yogurt, caster sugar, and vanilla until well mixed.

2 Beat the egg white until it forms stiff peaks. Fold gradually into the cheese mixture.

3 Line *coeur à la crème* moulds (heart-shaped ceramic moulds with holes in the base) with muslin or J-cloth and spoon in the mixture. If unavailable, use small yogurt or cream pots with holes pierced in the base. Leave to drain on a tray in the refrigerator for at least 12 hours.

4 To make the coulis, halve the passion fruits and scoop out the flesh. Rub the flesh through a sieve to remove the pips. Add the icing sugar to the purée and mix well.

5 Turn out the moulds onto a serving plate. Drizzle the sauce around the crème (about 1 tablespoon per person) and serve with soft fruits.

COEUR À LA CRÈME &
PASSION FRUIT

SPICY
KEDGEREE

SPICY KEDGEREE

10 MINUTES   20–30 MINUTES

INGREDIENTS

200G (7OZ) BASMATI RICE
1 TBSP OLIVE OIL
30G (1OZ) BUTTER
1 TBSP MILD CURRY POWDER
6 CARDAMOMS, SEEDS CRUSHED
2 TSP GROUND CUMIN
2 SHALLOTS, FINELY CHOPPED
200G (7OZ) FISH (COD, WHITING, OR HAKE),
BONED, SKINNED, & FLAKED
LARGE PINCH OF GROUND SAFFRON
500ML (17FL OZ) FISH STOCK (SEE PAGE 185)
2 EGGS, HARD BOILED, PEELED, & CHOPPED
2 TBSP CRÈME FRAÎCHE
LUMPFISH ROE & SPRIGS FRESH PARSLEY
TO GARNISH

1 Wash the rice in a sieve under cold running water until the water runs completely clear.

2 Heat the olive oil and butter in a saucepan. Add the curry powder, cardamom, cumin, and shallots. Cook gently, stirring, for 5 minutes, until the shallots are softened.

3 Add the rice, fish, and saffron and stir until the rice is completely coated in the oil, then add the stock. Bring to the boil, stir, and then turn the heat to very low. Cover tightly and cook undisturbed for 8 minutes.

4 Remove the rice from the heat, stir once, and fluff up with a fork. The rice should be separated into grains and *al dente*.

5 Add the eggs to the rice and fish mixture, then add the crème fraîche. Stir well. Serve with a garnish of lumpfish roe and several sprigs of fresh parsley.

COOK'S TIP
The kedgeree can be made the day before and refrigerated. Reheat it in a moderate oven for 15 minutes before serving.

RICH LEMON CURD

10 MINUTES   30–40 MINUTES

INGREDIENTS

8 EGGS: YOLKS ONLY
250G (8OZ) CASTER SUGAR
5 LEMONS, JUICE & GRATED ZEST
150G (5OZ) UNSALTED BUTTER, CHILLED
& IN PIECES
3 x 250G (8OZ) JARS

1 Place the egg yolks and sugar in a double boiler, or a heatproof bowl over a saucepan of simmering water. Gently whisk for about 10 minutes, until the mixture begins to thicken.

2 Whisk in the lemon juice and zest, then gradually add the butter, a piece at a time. Continue to whisk for about 20–30 minutes, until thickened. Do not allow the mixture to boil or it will separate.

3 Spoon the mixture into sterilized jars. Cover the tops of the jars with discs of waxed paper, and tightly seal them. Leave to cool, then refrigerate the jars until needed. Serve with slightly warmed brioche.

COOK'S TIP
Lemon curd will keep for up to 3 months in the refrigerator.

WINTER BREAKFAST FOR 6

BUBBLE & SQUEAK

🥄 20 MINUTES 🍲 45 MINUTES

INGREDIENTS
750G (1½ LB) POTATOES, PEELED
1 TBSP OLIVE OIL, PLUS EXTRA FOR DRIZZLING
90G (3OZ) SMOKED PANCETTA OR SMOKED
STREAKY BACON, DERINDED & SLICED
2 LEEKS, THINLY SLICED
375G (12OZ) SAVOY CABBAGE, SHREDDED
SALT & PEPPER TO TASTE
100G (3½ OZ) BUTTER, IN PIECES

COOK'S TIP
This may be prepared, but not baked, a day ahead. Cover the baking dish with clingfilm and refrigerate overnight. Bake for an extra 5–10 minutes.

1 Preheat oven to 220°C/450°F/Gas 8. Place the potatoes in a saucepan of cold water, bring to the boil, cover, and simmer for 12 minutes, until cooked.

2 Meanwhile, heat the olive oil in a large frying pan and cook the pancetta for 10 minutes, until crisp. Drain on kitchen paper.

3 Cook the leeks and cabbage in a large pan of salted boiling water for 4 minutes, until *al dente*. Refresh under cold water and drain.

4 When the potatoes are cooked, drain and then mash well. Stir in the pancetta, leeks, and cabbage, and adjust seasoning.

5 Spoon the mixture into a large greased baking dish, dot with butter, and drizzle with olive oil. Bake in the oven for about 20–25 minutes, until brown on top.

HERBED
TOMATOES

BUBBLE &
SQUEAK

CREAMY
SCRAMBLED EGGS

HERBED TOMATOES

⏱ 5 MINUTES 🍲 20 MINUTES

INGREDIENTS
3 LARGE TOMATOES (PREFERABLY BEEFSTEAK)
1 TBSP CLEAR HONEY
1 TBSP EACH FRESH THYME & PARSLEY,
FINELY CHOPPED
30G (1OZ) BUTTER
SALT & PEPPER TO TASTE

1 Preheat oven to 220°C/450°F/Gas 8. Cut each tomato in half and remove the core from the centre. Place in an ovenproof dish, cut side up.

2 Combine the remaining ingredients in a mixing bowl. Spread the herb mixture over the tomato halves and bake in the oven for 15–20 minutes, until crisp on top.

COOK'S TIP
The tomatoes can be cooked in the oven with the Bubble and Squeak (see opposite).

CREAMY SCRAMBLED EGGS

⏱ 5 MINUTES 🍲 4 MINUTES

INGREDIENTS
12 EGGS
SALT & PEPPER TO TASTE
60G (2OZ) BUTTER
90ML (3FL OZ) WHIPPING CREAM

1 Lightly beat the eggs and seasoning until mixed but not foamy.

2 Melt the butter in a frying pan or saucepan over a low heat. Add the eggs and stir constantly until they start to thicken and are the consistency of soft whipped cream.

3 Remove from the heat and add the cream. Stir well. Serve immediately.

COOK'S TIP
It is always best to cook with eggs that are at room temperature.

ORANGE & LIME MARMALADE

⏱ 1 HOUR 15 MINUTES 🍲 6 HOURS 30 MINUTES ⏲ 6 HOURS COOLING

INGREDIENTS
8 ORANGES (PREFERABLY SEVILLE)
6 LIMES
3 LEMONS
2.5KG (5LB) SUGAR OR PRESERVING SUGAR

COOK'S TIPS
If you have a sugar thermometer, the temperature needed for setting is 104°C/219°F. Let the marmalade stand for 15 minutes and stir before potting to prevent the fruit rising to top. The recipe makes about 4kg (8lb) of marmalade.

1 Place the whole oranges, limes, and lemons in a large saucepan or preserving pan and cover with water. Bring to the boil, cover, and simmer over a very low heat for 6 hours. Leave to cool, covered, for a further 6 hours.

2 Cut the fruits in half, remove and discard the pips, and chop coarsely. Reserve 1.25 litres (2 pints) of the liquid in the pan.

3 Add the chopped fruits and sugar to the pan and place over a medium heat, stirring constantly, until the sugar dissolves. Bring to the boil.

4 After 15 minutes, test the mixture to see if the marmalade is ready: place a teaspoon of the mixture on a chilled plate and put it in the freezer for one minute – if the liquid gels on the plate, it is ready. If not, repeat the test every 2 minutes until it has set (it may take up to 30 minutes). Remove the marmalade from the heat.

5 Pour the marmalade into sterilized jars. Cover the tops of the jars with discs of waxed paper and tightly seal them. Store in a cool, dry place.

LUNCH

RELAXING MEALS IN THE MIDDLE OF THE DAY ARE ALL TOO OFTEN NEGLECTED THANKS TO THE HECTIC PACE OF MODERN LIVING. YET THEY CAN BE ONE OF LIFE'S GREAT PLEASURES, AS OUR APPETITES ARE AT THEIR SHARPEST AT NOON. THE WEEKEND BECOMES IDEAL FOR A SIMPLE BUT DELICIOUS MEAL WITH EITHER FAMILY OR FRIENDS. ONCE FOOD AND WINE HAVE BEEN SAVOURED, PLENTY OF TIME IS LEFT FOR INDULGING IN LEISURELY CONVERSATION, A WALK, OR EVEN A SIESTA.

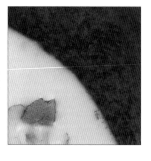

For a tempting exotic lunch party, team the interesting textures and spicy tastes of the Oriental Flavours menu (page 52), with brilliant flowers and vibrant colours (right).

VIBRANT

Never neglect colour: it plays a major part

THE COLOUR of both food and tableware affects our enjoyment of meals more than we might imagine: vibrant colours set our taste buds tingling. Entertain colourfully and your meals will always be memorable.

Phlox

Ranunculus

Rose

Selaginella

FLOATING FLOWERS
Place low bowls of floating, brightly coloured flowers on the table where they will not interrupt your view. Choose flowers and foliage in vivid colours that contrast and clash excitingly with each other. Here, I have used the fern selaginella and roses in a black glass etched bowl.

CONTRAST
Note how much the effect changes when flowers of different colours are used. Try alternative varieties to tie in with your own setting.

1 Trim off the foliage stems, leaving about 1cm (½in). If necessary, make small bunches by tying 3–4 stems together.

2 Cut each of the flower stems immediately below the base of its flowerhead. Take care not to dislodge the petals.

3 Almost fill a shallow bowl with water. Place foliage bunches in first, then position your flowers (above left).

in enjoying food

FLOWER SETTINGS
Small bowls with roses, gerbera, and fern leaves, are arranged at each place setting to echo the main display.

BOLD NAPKINS
When tied in a bow with pink wire-edged ribbon, brilliant blue linen napkins are brightened still further.

PATTERNED TABLECLOTH
As demonstrated by the tapestry-like cloth that sets the colour theme for the china, tablecloths need not always form a neutral backdrop.

SEASCAPE

Nothing sharpens the appetite more than

VISUALIZE SAILS on a glittering sea, and whitewashed houses in the sun. Then create this sparkling atmosphere using the sunbleached hues borrowed from land and seascapes.

PAPER RIBBON NAPKIN RINGS
Follow through the seaside theme by making napkin rings in sea-green pleated paper ribbon.

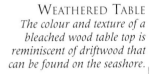

1 Cut a 1m (39in) length of paper ribbon for each person. Wind the ribbon twice around two fingers (this loop will hold the napkin). Thread one end through the loop.

2 The two ends should be roughly equal in length. Keeping two fingers in the loop to preserve its shape, tie a simple up-and-over knot with the ends.

3 Thread one end between the knot and the loop and pull tight. Fan out and neaten the knot. Choose a neat diagonal or a v-shaped cut, and trim the ends to the required length.

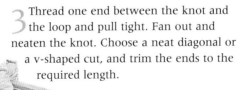

Trim ends in preferred shape

a walk beside the sea

VEGETABLE POT
Fill a small straight-sided terracotta pot with Spanish moss and nestle a vegetable, such as miniature broccoli or the cauliflower seen here, on top.

SHELL SALT CELLAR
Use a sea shell as a receptacle for coarse sea salt. Mother-of-pearl lined mussel shells would be suitable too.

GLASSES
Frosted glasses harmonize perfectly with the muted colours of the tableware.

DECORATIVE VEGETABLE DISPLAY

Vegetables and foliage nestling in a simple painted box make an eye-catching and original decoration for the centre of the dining table or a side table. Bleached whites associate with sea-blue-greens and washed wood tones, to continue our seascape theme (pages 48–9); from the huge selection that is available, choose vegetables to match your colour scheme.

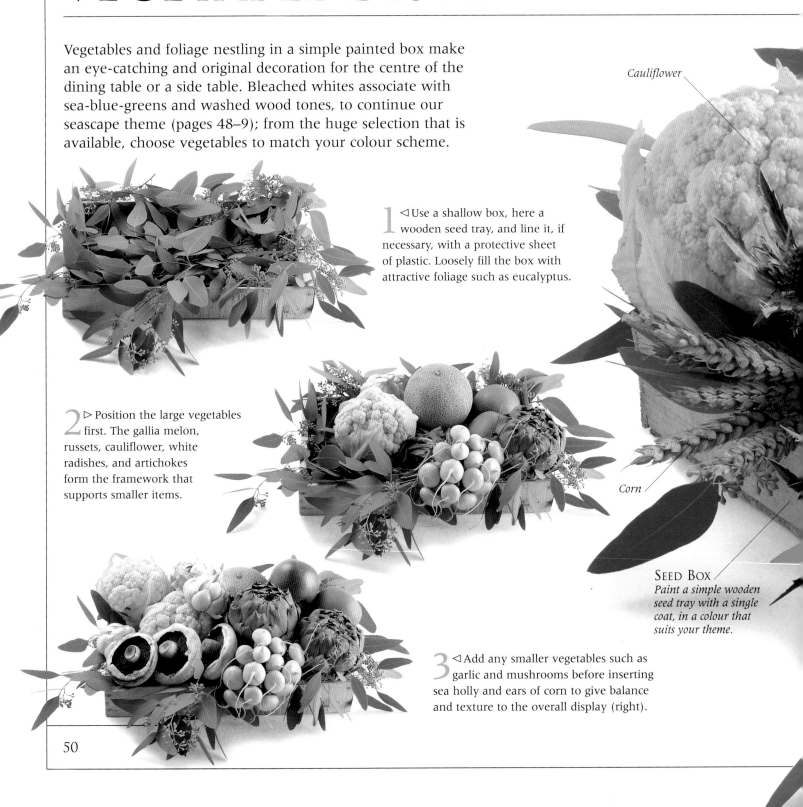

Cauliflower

1 ◁ Use a shallow box, here a wooden seed tray, and line it, if necessary, with a protective sheet of plastic. Loosely fill the box with attractive foliage such as eucalyptus.

2 ▷ Position the large vegetables first. The gallia melon, russets, cauliflower, white radishes, and artichokes form the framework that supports smaller items.

Corn

SEED BOX
Paint a simple wooden seed tray with a single coat, in a colour that suits your theme.

3 ◁ Add any smaller vegetables such as garlic and mushrooms before inserting sea holly and ears of corn to give balance and texture to the overall display (right).

Russet Apple

Artichoke

Melon

Garlic

White Radish

Eucalyptus

TEXTURE & CONTRAST
*The dominant rounded
forms of large vegetables are
offset by contrasting spikes
of corn and sea holly, and
bobbled eucalyptus flowers.*

Mushroom

Sea Holly

MENUS

There is no greater luxury than lingering

ALFRESCO LUNCH

Here's a combination of simple flavours that spell out summer sunshine. Each of the courses is quick to prepare. *Serves 6*

FIG & FETA SALAD
This impressive dish is light, easy to make, and a glorious feast for both the eye and palate.

FRESH PAN-FRIED SARDINES
You will be transported to a cool vine-covered courtyard on the edge of the glittering sea with this zesty mix of fish and herbs.

AROMATIC FRUIT SALAD
Finish off with a taste of the sun in the form of these exotic fruit-packed paper parcels.

DRINKS
Enjoy the aromatic crispness of a white Rioja with this summer menu.

PLANNING NOTES
The aromatic fruit salad can be arranged, ready for baking, well in advance of the meal. Bear in mind that preparing paper parcels for more than 12 can take time. The fig and feta salad can be made in quantity up to a couple of hours in advance. Prepare the sauce for the sardines up to 12 hours before you need it, but cook the fish at the last moment. *See pages 54–5 for recipes.*

ORIENTAL FLAVOURS

This menu is characterized by the sharp spicy flavours that typify Eastern cuisine. *Serves 6*

TIGER PRAWN SOUP
Once tasted, you'll recognize that prawns and coconut are made for each other.

ORIENTAL PARCELS WITH SPICY SAUCE
Crispy filo parcels of thinly sliced pork and crunchy cashews, complemented by a tangy sauce.

GINGER SORBET
Being sweet vegetables, carrots work well in this exotic ice with ginger. The sorbet is temptingly served in edible ginger baskets.

DRINKS
Saki offered warm is the ideal oriental accompaniment. Have jasmine tea as a non-alcoholic alternative.

PLANNING NOTES
Make the ginger sorbet up to six weeks in advance – a great stand-by for unexpected visitors. The ginger baskets will keep in an airtight tin for up to two weeks. Although the oriental parcels take some time to assemble, the prawn soup and ginger sorbet are simplicity itself to make. The parcels are best cooked and eaten immediately, so can be unsuitable for large numbers. *See pages 56–7 for recipes.*

over a lazy lunch

WINTER FARE

The food we enjoy varies with the seasons:
winter is a time for hearty dishes. This is a menu of
satisfying and sophisticated cold-weather treats.
Serves 12

POTATO & BACON SALAD
*Add tiny quantities of truffles to this salad to make it extra
special; potatoes are superb at taking on their flavour.*

PEPPERED LAMB
*Pepper livens the taste buds and enhances the flavour of the
tender sweet meat.*

WINTER COMPOTE WITH PRUNE ICE CREAM
*Dried fruits have an intensity of flavour that is just right in
the depths of winter. This medley is delicious served with
prune ice cream.*

DRINKS
The softness of red Merlot wine makes it ideal for this lunch.

PLANNING NOTES
The ice cream can be made up to six weeks in advance.
Make the compote two days ahead as it improves over time.
Prepare the potato and bacon salad the day before, especially
if using truffles, to allow the flavours to develop; arrange
it on salad leaves at the last minute. The sauce for the
peppered lamb can also be made a day ahead, if necessary;
keep it covered in the refrigerator. The lamb is best eaten
immediately after cooking; always use the finest quality meat.
See pages 58–9 for recipes.

SEASIDE FAVOURITES

The association with sparkling seas and
whitewashed clapboard houses makes these
dishes irresistible. *Serves 6*

FISH CAKES WITH HERB SAUCE
*No heaviness here: just wonderful fresh fish with mayonnaise
and herbs, fried to crisp perfection and accompanied by a
delicate herb sauce.*

BLUEBERRY TART
*The family recipe of my friend, Mary Lublin, combines cooked
and raw blueberries in a sharp, not too sweet sauce. The fruit
explodes with flavour as you eat it.*

DRINKS
*Iced tea, a refreshing American speciality, is an ideal choice,
served with or without lemon.*

PLANNING NOTES
The pastry case for the blueberry tart can be made two days
in advance and stored in an airtight container. For the fish
cakes, prepare the fish mixture and sauce several hours ahead
of the meal and keep refrigerated. The fish cakes can be fried
up to one hour before serving, if you keep them warm.
See pages 60–1 for recipes.

ALFRESCO LUNCH FOR 6

FIG & FETA SALAD
☑ 20 MINUTES

INGREDIENTS
3 LARGE TOMATOES (PREFERABLY BEEFSTEAK)
175G (6OZ) FETA CHEESE, CRUMBLED
6 SPRIGS BASIL, FINELY CHOPPED
90G (3OZ) BLACK OLIVES, PITTED
8 FIGS
2 COURGETTES
2 TBSP BALSAMIC VINEGAR, PLUS
EXTRA TO SERVE
SALT & PEPPER TO TASTE
WATERCRESS TO GARNISH

1 Peel and quarter the tomatoes, remove and discard the cores and seeds, and finely chop the flesh. Place in a salad bowl with the feta, basil, and olives. Dice 6 of the figs and add them to the bowl.

2 Cut the courgettes in half and shave them lengthways into thin ribbon strips, using a potato peeler. Roll 18 lengths into tight cylinders and set aside. Finely chop the remaining strips and add to the bowl.

3 Add the vinegar and seasoning to the salad and toss well. Cover and refrigerate until required (preferably no longer than 4 hours).

4 Just before serving, place a plain round pastry cutter – about 9cm (3½in) in diameter – on a serving plate. Pile the salad into centre of the cutter and press down lightly. Remove the cutter carefully and repeat for the remaining servings.

5 Slice the remaining figs and serve with the salad. Arrange 3 reserved courgette rolls on top of each salad, garnish with watercress, and sprinkle over a little balsamic vinegar.

COOK'S TIPS
The salad can be varied according to the season. Always use brightly coloured ingredients; cut them finely so they hold together in the mould.

FRESH PAN-FRIED SARDINES
☑ 10 MINUTES   ☐ 10 MINUTES   ☐ 30 MINUTES SOAKING

INGREDIENTS
60G (2OZ) RAISINS
18 SARDINES
5 TBSP PLAIN FLOUR
SALT & PEPPER TO TASTE
3 TBSP OLIVE OIL
3 GARLIC CLOVES, SKINS LEFT ON, CRUSHED
UNDER THE FLAT OF A KNIFE
6 SHALLOTS, FINELY CHOPPED
3 BAY LEAVES
125ML (4FL OZ) RED WINE VINEGAR
4 TBSP PINE NUTS, LIGHTLY TOASTED
MIXED SALAD LEAVES & FOCACCIA (SEE
PAGE 186) TO SERVE

1 Soak the raisins in water for 30 minutes. Gut and scale the sardines, if necessary, and remove their heads. Toss lightly in seasoned flour.

2 Heat the olive oil in a large frying pan. Add the garlic and sardines and fry gently for about 1½ minutes each side. Transfer the sardines to a warmed dish to keep hot in the oven.

3 To make the sauce, add the shallots and bay leaves to the same pan and cook over a medium heat until the

shallots are just softened. Add the vinegar, pine nuts, and raisins and cook until bubbling. Discard the garlic.

4 To serve, arrange the sardines on a bed of mixed salad leaves and pour the hot sauce over them. Serve with home-made Focaccia.

COOK'S TIP
These sardines are also delicious cooked for the same length of time on the barbecue, but be sure not to overcook them.

FRESH PAN-FRIED
SARDINES

AROMATIC FRUIT SALAD

20 MINUTES   10 MINUTES

INGREDIENTS

1 LARGE RIPE MANGO, PEELED

1 LARGE PINEAPPLE, PEELED

3 PASSION FRUITS (OPTIONAL)

2 LIMES, JUICE & GRATED ZEST

6 SHAKES OF ANGOSTURA BITTERS

6 PINCHES EACH OF GROUND CLOVES, ALLSPICE
& BLACK PEPPER

4 TBSP SOFT DARK BROWN SUGAR

6 TBSP DARK RUM (OPTIONAL)

1 Preheat oven to 200°C/400°F/Gas 6. Cut the mango and pineapple flesh into chunks. Halve the passion fruits, if using, and scoop out their flesh together with the seeds.

2 Cut 6 pieces of baking parchment, 30cm (12in) square. Fold each square diagonally. Open out and lay 1 piece of paper on a plate. Place one-sixth of the fruit on one side of the fold. Sprinkle a dash of the lime juice and zest, the bitters, and a pinch of each of

the spices. Add 2 teaspoons of sugar and 1 tablespoon of rum, if using.

3 Fold the paper over the fruits to enclose, then double fold the edges. Pleat the folded edges of the triangle. Place on a baking sheet. Repeat to make the remaining 5 parcels.

4 Bake in the oven for 10 minutes. Serve the unopened parcels with fruit sorbet or ice cream, allowing your guests to tear them open at the table.

ORIENTAL FLAVOURS FOR 6

TIGER PRAWN SOUP

 15 MINUTES 15 MINUTES

INGREDIENTS

12–18 RAW TIGER PRAWNS, ABOUT 250G (8OZ)
400ML (14FL OZ) WATER
400ML (14FL OZ) COCONUT MILK
1 TBSP FISH SAUCE
2 TSP SUGAR
1½ LIMES, JUICE & GRATED ZEST
3 FRESH GREEN CHILLIES, DESEEDED
& FINELY CHOPPED
3 STALKS LEMON GRASS, FINELY CHOPPED
2 GARLIC CLOVES, CRUSHED
2.5CM (1IN) PIECE OF GALANGAL,
THINLY SLICED
6 KAFFIR LIME LEAVES (PREFERABLY
FRESH), TORN
1½ TBSP TAMARIND PULP (OPTIONAL)
⅓ –½ CUCUMBER, CUT IN MATCHSTICKS
3 TBSP FRESH CORIANDER, COARSELY
CHOPPED, TO GARNISH

1 Prepare the prawns (see Step 1, page 94). Place the shells into a large saucepan with the water, coconut milk, fish sauce, sugar, lime juice, and chillies. Bring to the boil and simmer for 5 minutes. Strain and discard the prawn shells, returning the cooking liquid to the saucepan.

2 Add the lemon grass, garlic, galangal, lime leaves, lime zest, and tamarind, if using, and return to the boil. Simmer for 5 minutes.

3 Add the cucumber and prawns and cook for 2 more minutes. Serve in warmed soup bowls, and sprinkle with the coriander.

COOK'S TIPS

Galangal, kaffir lime leaves, and tamarind pulp are all available in Oriental grocery stores. Galangal can be replaced with a 1cm (½in) piece of fresh root ginger, peeled and very finely chopped. Use the grated zest of 2 limes instead of kaffir lime leaves, if necessary.

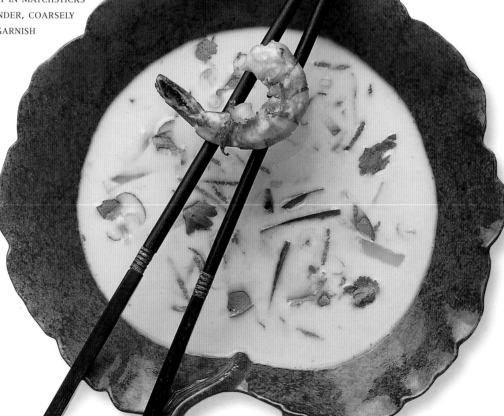

TIGER PRAWN
SOUP

ORIENTAL PARCELS WITH SPICY SAUCE

30 Minutes · 18 Minutes · 1 Hour Marinating

INGREDIENTS

1 TBSP FISH SAUCE
90ML (3FL OZ) OYSTER SAUCE
3 TBSP LIGHT SOY SAUCE
3 FRESH RED CHILLIES, DESEEDED
& FINELY CHOPPED
5 GARLIC CLOVES, FINELY CHOPPED
2.5CM (1IN) PIECE FRESH GINGER,
FINELY CHOPPED
225G (8OZ) PORK FILLET, WELL CHILLED
2 TSP VEGETABLE OIL
4 SHALLOTS, FINELY CHOPPED
125G (4OZ) UNSALTED CASHEW NUTS,
COARSELY CHOPPED
24 SHEETS FILO PASTRY, APPROXIMATELY
30 x 17CM (12 x 7IN), ABOUT 250G (8OZ)
90G (3OZ) BUTTER, MELTED
2 TBSP SESAME OIL
½ TSP GROUND CINNAMON
¼ TSP GROUND NUTMEG
2 TSP GROUND CORIANDER
125ML (4FL OZ) WATER
2 TBSP SHERRY VINEGAR
1 LIME, JUICE & GRATED ZEST
2 TSP SUGAR

1 To make the marinade, combine the fish sauce, 3 tablespoons of the oyster sauce, 1 tablespoon of the soy sauce, 2 chillies, 2 garlic cloves, and the ginger. Cut the pork into very thin slices and place in a shallow non-metallic dish. Pour over the marinade, cover, and leave to marinate in the refrigerator for 1 hour.

2 Heat the vegetable oil in a wok or frying pan and stir-fry the shallots until pale golden. Add the pork with the marinade, and the nuts, and continue to fry until the pork is golden. Leave to cool.

3 Preheat oven to 180°C/350°F/Gas 4. Lay out 1 sheet of filo pastry, brush lightly with melted butter, lay a second sheet crosswise over it, and brush this with butter. Turn the pastry over. Place about a tablespoon of the pork and nut mixture in the centre.

4 Gather up the pastry around the meat, twist into a parcel, and place it on a greased baking sheet. Make 11 more parcels in this way. Bake for about 15–18 minutes, until golden.

5 Meanwhile, make the spicy sauce. Heat the sesame oil a small pan. Add the remaining garlic and the cinnamon, nutmeg, and coriander, and brown lightly.

6 Remove the pan from the heat and add the water, remaining soy sauce, oyster sauce, vinegar, lime juice and zest, and sugar. Stir. Return to the boil and simmer for 4–5 minutes. Serve the Oriental parcels with the sauce drizzled over, accompanied by mangetouts and baby asparagus.

COOK'S TIP
For an attractive presentation, tie the tops of the parcels with 2 strands of chives before baking.

GINGER SORBET

15 Minutes · 10 Minutes · 8 Hours Chilling

INGREDIENTS

300ML (½ PT) WATER
300G (10OZ) CASTER SUGAR
500ML (17FL OZ) CARROT JUICE
2 LIMES, JUICE & GRATED ZEST
5–7½ CM (2–3IN) PIECE OF FRESH GINGER,
PEELED & FINELY CHOPPED
1 EGG, WHITE ONLY
12 GINGER BASKETS (SEE BRANDY SNAPS
COOK'S TIP, PAGE 182)

1 Heat the water and sugar in a saucepan over a moderate heat. Bring to the boil, stirring until the syrup has dissolved and is clear. Add the carrot juice, lime juice and zest, and ginger. Leave to cool, then refrigerate for 2 hours, until chilled.

2 Pour the mixture into a freezer-proof container, cover, and freeze for 3 hours, stirring at the end of each hour. On the final stirring, lightly beat the egg white, then fold it into the mixture. Refreeze for at least 3 hours.

3 Transfer the sorbet to the refrigerator 30 minutes before serving, to soften. Allow 2 scoops per person and serve in Ginger Baskets.

COOK'S TIP
If you have an ice cream maker, follow the manufacturer's instructions.

WINTER FARE FOR 12

POTATO & BACON SALAD

🥄 15 MINUTES 🍲 15 MINUTES ⬜ 12 HOURS MARINATING

INGREDIENTS
2 WHITE TRUFFLES, FRESH OR
BOTTLED (OPTIONAL)
2 TBSP OLIVE OIL
350G (12OZ) SMOKED PANCETTA OR SMOKED
STREAKY BACON, DERINDED & SLICED
1.25KG (2½LB) NEW POTATOES, SCRUBBED
6 SPRIGS FRESH MINT
150ML (¼PT) VINAIGRETTE (SEE PAGE 185)
GREEN SALAD LEAVES TO SERVE

1 If you are using fresh truffles, peel them the day before and reserve the peel. Keep the truffles wrapped and airtight in refrigerator until required.

2 Heat the oil in a frying pan. Add the bacon with the truffle peel, if using, and cook until golden. Remove the bacon and drain on kitchen paper. Discard the truffle peel.

3 Cook the potatoes and mint in a large saucepan of salted boiling water for about 12–15 minutes, until the potatoes are just cooked. Drain.

4 When the potatoes are cool enough to handle, cut into ½cm (¼in) slices. Place in a large, non-metallic dish. Sprinkle with the bacon and pour over the Vinaigrette. Cover and marinate overnight in the refrigerator.

5 Slice the truffles very thinly. To serve, arrange the potatoes and bacon with the Vinaigrette on a bed of salad leaves, and add the truffle slices.

COOK'S TIP
If using bottled truffles, use some of the oil to make the Vinaigrette.

PEPPERED LAMB

🥄 30 MINUTES 🍲 55 MINUTES

INGREDIENTS
30G (1OZ) DRIED CEPS
500ML (17FL OZ) HOT WATER
60G (2OZ) UNSALTED BUTTER
8 ANCHOVY FILLETS, FINELY CHOPPED
4 TBSP OLIVE OIL
2 BONED & TRIMMED LOINS OF LAMB, ABOUT
1.25KG (2½LB) EACH, WITH BONES RESERVED
2 GARLIC CLOVES, SKINS LEFT ON, CRUSHED
UNDER THE FLAT OF A KNIFE
750ML (1¼PT) RED WINE
4 TBSP MIXED PEPPERCORNS, CRUSHED
4 TBSP FRESH MINT, FINELY CHOPPED
TAGLIATELLE & BRAISED CHICORY (SEE
PAGE 187) TO SERVE

COOK'S TIP
Unless you have a very large pan, you may find you need to cook the lamb in 2 pans.

1 To make the sauce, grind the ceps to a powder in an electric grinder or mortar and soak in the hot water for 30 minutes. Cream the butter and anchovies to a paste and refrigerate.

2 Meanwhile, heat 2 tablespoons of oil in a flameproof casserole. Add the lamb bones and garlic and cook until brown. Gradually add the wine and reduce to about 150ml (¼pint) over a gentle heat. Add the mushroom liquid and reduce by half. Discard the bones and garlic and reserve the sauce.

3 To prepare the lamb, brush with 1 tablespoon of oil and roll in the peppercorns mixed with mint. Heat the remaining oil in a large frying pan. Sear each loin all over until almost burnt. Reduce the heat and cook for a further 4–8 minutes, turning regularly, until just cooked inside. Transfer to a warmed dish; keep hot in a low oven.

4 To the same pan, add the reserved sauce and bring to the boil. Cut the anchovy butter into small pieces and add them gradually to the sauce, whisking after each addition, until the sauce is smooth.

5 Carve the lamb into 1cm (½in) slices and serve with the sauce, accompanied by Braised Chicory and tagliatelle.

BRAISED
CHICORY

PEPPERED
LAMB

WINTER COMPOTE WITH PRUNE ICE CREAM
15 MINUTES · 20 MINUTES · 8 HOURS CHILLING

INGREDIENTS
500G (1LB) PRUNES, PITTED
500ML (17FL OZ) PRUNE JUICE
125G (4OZ) CASTER SUGAR
5 LEMONS, JUICE & GRATED ZEST
600ML (1PT) WHIPPING CREAM, CHILLED
90ML (3FL OZ) ARMAGNAC OR BRANDY
375ML (12FL OZ) PORT OR MEDIUM DRY
SHERRY
10 CLOVES
24 DRIED PEAR HALVES
24 DRIED APRICOTS
12 DRIED FIGS

1 To make the ice cream, heat 300g (10oz) of the prunes, the prune juice, the sugar, and the juice of 3 lemons for about 10 minutes, until the prunes are soft. Liquidize in a blender, leave to cool, then refrigerate for at least 2 hours, until thoroughly chilled.

2 Whisk in the cream, grated zest of 3 lemons, and the Armagnac. Turn the mixture into a rigid freezerproof container, cover, and freeze for 3 hours, stirring at the end of each hour

(follow the manufacturer's instructions if you use an ice cream maker). Refreeze for at least 3 hours.

3 To make the compote, heat the port, cloves, the juice and zest of 2 lemons, and the dried fruits in a small saucepan. Do not allow to boil. Move to a basin, cover, and refrigerate overnight. Transfer the ice cream to the refrigerator 30 minutes before serving to soften. Serve the compote with 2 scoops of the ice cream per person.

SEASIDE FAVOURITES FOR 6

FISH CAKES WITH
HERB SAUCE

BLUEBERRY
TART

FISH CAKES WITH HERB SAUCE

25 MINUTES   20 MINUTES   1 HOUR CHILLING

INGREDIENTS

750G (1½ LB) SMOKED HADDOCK OR COD
125G (4OZ) LARGE COOKED PRAWNS
3 TBSP DILL, FINELY CHOPPED, PLUS
SPRIGS TO GARNISH
10 TBSP PARSLEY, FINELY CHOPPED
250ML (8FL OZ) CRÈME FRAÎCHE
4 TBSP MAYONNAISE
SALT & PEPPER TO TASTE
2 TSP DIJON MUSTARD
45G (1½ OZ) FRESH WHITE BREADCRUMBS
30G (1OZ) UNSALTED BUTTER
2 TBSP VEGETABLE OIL
LEMON WEDGES TO GARNISH

1 To make the fish cakes, place the fish in a saucepan, half cover with water, cover and simmer gently for 5–10 minutes, until tender. Drain and allow to cool. Flake the fish, discarding the skin and bones.

2 In a food processor, combine the fish, prawns, half of the dill, half of the parsley, 2 tablespoons of crème fraîche, the mayonnaise, and seasoning. Process for a few seconds, until the mixture is just combined. Cover and refrigerate for 1 hour.

3 Meanwhile, prepare the sauce: in a food processor, combine the remaining dill, parsley, and crème fraîche with the mustard and a little seasoning, until thickened. Put the mixture in a bowl, cover, and refrigerate until required.

4 Remove the fish cake mixture from the refrigerator. Divide the mixture into 12 round patties, about 2cm (¾ in) in depth. Roll them in breadcrumbs.

5 Divide the butter and oil between 2 heavy-based frying pans. Fry the fish cakes for about 10 minutes, until golden on both sides.

6 Serve hot with the chilled sauce and a green salad. Garnish with lemon wedges and dill sprigs.

BLUEBERRY TART

20 MINUTES   30 MINUTES

INGREDIENTS

375G (12OZ) SWEET SHORTCRUST PASTRY
(SEE PAGE 184)
750G (1½ LB) BLUEBERRIES
1½ LEMONS, JUICE & GRATED ZEST
30G (1OZ) CASTER SUGAR
1 TBSP CORNFLOUR, SIFTED
4 TBSP WATER
ICING SUGAR TO DUST
CRÈME FRAÎCHE TO SERVE

1 For the crust, roll out the pastry and press into a 25cm (10in) loose-bottomed fluted tart tin. Prick the bottom of the pastry all over with a fork then refrigerate for 30 minutes.

2 Preheat oven to 180°C/350°F/Gas 4. Line the dough with greaseproof paper, fill with dried beans, and bake for 15 minutes, until the pastry is just set. Remove the greaseproof paper and beans. Return to the oven for a further 15 minutes until golden. Allow to cool completely.

3 For the filling, heat half of the blueberries in a saucepan with the lemon juice and zest and sugar. Mix the cornflour with the water, then add to the blueberry mixture, stirring until well combined. Bring to the boil then simmer, covered, for about 5–10 minutes, stirring occasionally, until the fruit is soft.

4 Leave the blueberry mixture to cool for about 10 minutes, then stir in the remaining berries.

5 Place the pastry case on a serving plate and fill with the berry mixture. Leave to cool completely. Dust with icing sugar and serve with a large spoonful of crème fraîche.

COOK'S TIP
The cooked filling can be made with frozen blueberries, but 375g (12oz) should still be fresh.

DINNER

EVENING HAS TO BE THE OPTIMUM TIME TO ENTERTAIN. WORK AND OTHER DAYTIME ACTIVITIES ARE OVER, PEOPLE ARE ALL READY TO WIND DOWN AND ALLOW THE DAY'S PRESSURES TO RECEDE. APPETITES ARE KEEN AND WE CAN LOOK FORWARD TO BEING SOCIABLE. SO SEND OFF INVITATIONS, SELECT A TANTALIZING MENU, ADORN THE DINING TABLE, PREPARE SUMPTUOUS FOOD AND DRINKS, AND JOIN YOUR GUESTS IN STIMULATING CONVERSATION.

Prepare the Festive Celebration menu (page 74) for a rich and colourful Carnival party (right) at which you and all your guests wear masks.

CARNIVAL
Celebration is the elixir of the gods

CARNIVAL IS ALL about merrymaking, mystery, and intrigue, and colour always plays a large role. Here, I've used black and white, the colours of night and light, to create the atmosphere.

Use spectacles to plot position of eye-hole

FLOWER BOWL

Place two or three shallow bowls filled with flowers (see page 46 for technique) on the table for decoration. If you have other flower arrangements elsewhere, use some of the same flowers for floating; my choice was inspired by the epergne (pages 66–7).

HARLEQUIN MASKS

Simple to make and paint, these are designed to relate to the china. Lay one beside each place.

1 To make a template, plot a centre line. Use a plate to draw a 20cm (8in) long oval. Draw a design on one half, cut it out, fold along centre, trace other half.

2 Cut out the other side of the template, then use it to trace as many masks as you need onto stiff card. Cut them out. Use a craft knife to make eye-holes.

3 In a well-ventilated area, spray stripes of paint, first in one direction, then in another, to create diamonds. Finally, glue a painted stick to each mask.

White Dill *Phlox*

Rose

Spray stripes between two strips of card

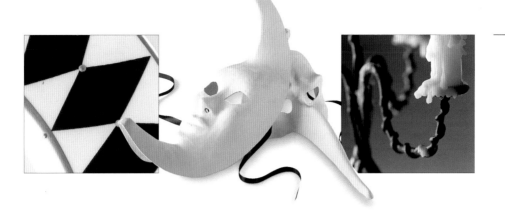

SILVER BOW
Lace-like silver ribbon tied in simple bows adds sparkle to this formal setting.

BLACK STONE TABLE
A dark surface like this stone (or a black tablecloth) forms a dramatic background for white place mats.

FLOWER BOWL
A soup bowl belonging to the same set of crockery makes an excellent showcase for flowers on the table.

GRAND CENTREPIECE

The epergne was a fashionable decoration for the centre of a dining table or a sideboard around the turn of the century. It was usually made of glass, often etched, with several tiers to hold a fountain of fruits, flowers, and sweetmeats. Here, I have improvised my own epergne with two glass cake stands and a small flared glass vase for a similarly effective display.

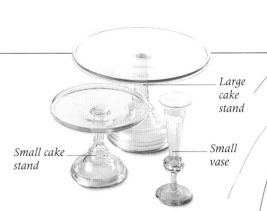

Large cake stand

Small cake stand

Small vase

1 Fix a small cake stand to the centre of a larger one using adhesive putty. Secure a vase or fluted glass, filled with water, to the small stand to form a tower.

2 Stick florists' prongs to the cake stands with adhesive putty. Attach small bunches of grapes to each end of several wires, then lay them across the stands.

3 Make sure the prongs are firm and in the correct position, before pushing small blocks of soaked floral foam onto them; the putty will not adhere to a wet surface.

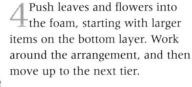

4 Push leaves and flowers into the foam, starting with larger items on the bottom layer. Work around the arrangement, and then move up to the next tier.

5 Arrange flowers and leaves in the vase at the top. Finally, add grass to create a fountain effect (main image), and finish by filling in any gaps.

FOUNTAIN OF SCENT
Elegant, softly bending stems of bear grass create the fountain effect, while the perfume of the roses gives further pleasure.

Bear Grass

Queen Anne's Lace

Phlox

White Rose

COLOUR SCHEME
Let the colour theme of your tableware influence your flower choice. I chose a froth of white with dark red and green to offset the black and white dinner service on page 64.

Grapes

TOWER OF GLASS
My improvised epergne stands firm on its broad glass base. Always be sure your tower is well balanced.

Philodendron

Pink Rose

FIRESIDE

"... intimate delights, fireside enjoyments,

GOOD FOOD in an atmosphere of warmth and comfort gives rise to superb conversation. Lighted candles and a crackling fire ensure an enjoyable supper.

CANDLE BASKET

Flowers, seeds, nuts, and spices mingle with similarly coloured candles in this box of delight. Never leave lit candles unattended.

TIMBER TABLE
This roughly hewn timber table is a good foil for the other warm, earthy textures.

1 Line three sections of a cutlery basket with plastic. Place four candles at random, securing with adhesive putty. Tie a bundle of cinnamon with raffia.

2 Cut wet foam slices to fit the plastic-lined sections, slicing curves for the candles where necessary. Fill the unlined sections with pecans and lychees, and position the cinnamon.

3 Push fresh roses and cone-flowers, with stems cut to 2.5cm (1in) long, into the wet foam to form a dense cover. Fill in with nuts and lychees, to complete the display (top). Dampen the foam so the flowers last.

home born happiness"

WILLIAM COWPER 1731–1800

CINNAMON CANDLE

Stand a candle with a cinnamon paling at each place. To make the paling, tie a loop at the middle of a length of string, then tie the sticks on behind. Make a bow through the loop when the paling is long enough.

CUTLERY REST

To encourage informality, use the same cutlery for all the savoury dishes. A tripod of cinnamon sticks tied with string forms an attractive resting place for the cutlery between courses.

SPRING

This bright enchanted time of joy reborn

SPRING SKIES, flowers, and young leaves, with their fresh clear colours, give a mouthwatering backdrop to light and delicate meals.

Cut the marbled paper into smaller sections or fold to suit your settings

MARBLED PAPER PLACE CARDS

Make highly individual place names or menu cards by marbling paper in colours to match your setting. Marbling paints are available from craft shops.

1 Half fill a shallow basin with water and add 3 tablespoons of vinegar. Using a pipette, drip in 6 drops of your first colour.

2 Drip in about twice as many drops of your second colour, then add a third colour on top of each of these drops.

3 Vary the number of colours (and amounts) as you wish. Spin the colours gently into a pattern using a skewer.

4 Take a piece of non-plastic coated, preferably porous paper. Ensure that the whole sheet will fit flat in the basin.

5 Place the paper flat on the water; it will curl almost immediately. Remove, lay face up to dry, and then iron flat.

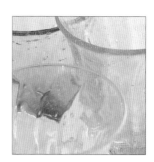

COLOURS OF SPRING
Mixing and matching fresh-coloured plates gives the table a spring-like appearance.

MARBLED PLACE NAMES
Marbled name cards draw together the elements on the table, echoing the colours of the tableware.

FRESH FLOWERS
Single tulip stems in jars are striking when arranged alongside candles chosen to match the crockery.

A TABLE DISPLAY FOR SPRING

The first flowers of spring cause a *frisson* of excitement, and they simply beg to be displayed. A Turkish miniature inspired this table arrangement of candles with specimen vases that show off the waxy beauty of tulips, the archetypal spring flower. Sit a single vase beside each place if table space is limited.

1 Many tulips can be "opened" by furling back their petals to give a lily-like effect. To do this, invert the base of the petal, just above the bottom of the flowerhead.

2 Taking care not to bruise the petals, continue to furl them back, gently easing them out with your fingers. Peel back all petals, including the inner ones.

Double Tulip

SPECIMEN VASE
Each teardrop-shaped vase in frosted glass holds just one or two tulip stems.

TRAY
A painted wooden tray contains all the vases and candles and provides them with a steady base.

FLOWERS
*Fresh spring yellow, white,
pastel pink, and lime green
illuminate this arrangement
and enhance the table
setting on pages 70–1.*

Single Tulip

CANDLES & HOLDERS
*Tulip-shaped glass holders are
most appropriate for the candles,
themselves in spring colours of
pink, green, and yellow.*

INDIVIDUAL
ARRANGEMENTS
*If your table is too
small to hold a tray,
two tulip stems in a
specimen vase beside
each place setting is
just as decorative.*

MENUS 1

"A good dinner and feasting reconciles

FESTIVE CELEBRATION

It's party time. If you cannot be in Rio de Janeiro, Venice, or New Orleans, recreate your own carnival celebrations. Dress up, put on masks, live the part!
Serves 6

SEARED PEARS & PARMA HAM
Pears are an unusual partner for Parma ham; an elegant mix of the simple and the glamorous.

SCALLOPS WITH CHARD
Subtle flavours and textures vie with each other for precedence.

CHOCOLATE TART
Certainly not for the weak, this tart will keep the most hardened of chocoholics gloriously happy.

DRINKS
Serve a good white Burgundy with the starter and main courses, and the Rhône Muscat, Beaumes-des-Venise, to accompany the chocolate tart.

PLANNING NOTES
Make the chocolate tart a day in advance. As it is very rich, it is fortunate that you can store any leftovers in the refrigerator for up to four days. The seared pears can also be prepared a day in advance and kept covered and refrigerated, but serve the Parma ham at room temperature. This recipe can easily be scaled up or down depending on the number of guests. Prepare the chard for the main meal an hour or so in advance, and heat it through while the scallops are cooking. *See pages 80–1 for recipes.*

LAVISH PARTY

You will be fêted when you serve this sumptuous menu that is rounded off with a light dessert.
Serves 12

CRAB TARTLETS WITH LEEK PURÉE
The leek and sherry purée makes an excellent accompaniment to the creamy crab tartlets.

DUCK WITH KUMQUATS
This variation on the traditional duck and orange recipe has a tangy sweet-sour sauce made with sliced kumquats.

SUMMER FRUITS WITH CRÈME FRAÎCHE
A glorious summer dessert, which is simple and most delicious.

DRINKS
Drink a good lightly chilled Verdicchio with the crab tarts, and a fruity cru *Beaujolais such as Brouilly or Fleurie with the duck. Try a Pineau de Charentes with the summer fruits.*

PLANNING NOTES
All these dishes can be prepared in part some hours in advance. Make the leek purée, and keep covered and refrigerated prior to serving, then heat it through on the hob. Tarts baked earlier the same day can be heated through in a moderate oven. Make the kumquat sauce and sear the duck breasts ahead of time, then refrigerate both until needed. Reheat the sauce while the duck is cooking. Prepare the crème fraîche mix and cover the fruits in advance, but grill immediately before eating. *See pages 82–3 for recipes.*

everyone" SAMUEL PEPYS 1663–1703

INTIMATE DINNER

A very special dinner for two, with the luxury of lobster as a main course. *Serves 2*

HERB OMELETTE WITH CAVIAR
Feather-light with a hint of truffle and a sprinkling of caviar.

LOBSTER WITH ROAST FIGS
The combination of flavours and textures is sublime. This dish also looks wonderful.

ORANGE & GRAPEFRUIT SORBETS
A pair of sorbets with unexpected ingredients.

DRINKS
Vintage Champagne followed by more Champagne. For the non-fizzy-minded, choose a grand *or* premier cru *Chablis as an alternative.*

PLANNING NOTES
The sorbets can be made up to six weeks in advance. The sauce for the lobster can be made up to four hours ahead and reheated. Have all the ingredients at the ready for the omelette, which needs to be eaten as soon as it is made. The starter and main course are best for two people, but the sorbets can be made for more than two batches and used as required. *See pages 84–5 for recipes.*

EXOTIC EVENING

All these dishes are subtly, yet interestingly, spiced to give a well-balanced exotic menu. *Serves 6*

PEPPERED SCALLOPS
Two colourful sauces accompany the peppery scallops.

LAMB TAGINE WITH COUSCOUS
Tender young lamb stuffed with a piquant-sweet mix of spices, herbs, and prunes.

COCONUT & SAFFRON ICE CREAM
A dreamy, creamy concoction with flavours and textures that are irresistible.

DRINKS
An oaked, buttery New World Chardonnay with the scallops, and a full, rich, spicy Australian Shiraz with the tagine, are ideal. Serve a chilled sweet white port with the ice cream.

PLANNING NOTES
The ice cream can be made up to six weeks ahead. Prepare the stuffing for the lamb tagine in advance, if necessary. The two sauces for the scallops can be prepared ahead of time, kept covered with clingfilm in the refrigerator, then heated through for serving. *See pages 86–7 for recipes.*

MENUS 2

"Woe to the cook whose sauce has no sting"

SPRING DINNER

Fresh, clean flavours of spring are captured in this irresistible menu. *Serves 6*

ROCKET SOUP
Wonderful rocket is at its sweetest, tangiest best in spring.

TARRAGON CHICKEN
Here, grilled chicken breasts are laced with a tempting tarragon sauce.

LIME & MINT MOULD
A cool, fragrant end to a dinner, which looks beautiful too.

DRINKS
A lightly oaked Chardonnay would be a perfect accompaniment to this menu. End with a faintly sweet Gewürztraminer.

PLANNING NOTES
The lime and mint mould can be prepared up to two days in advance and kept in the refrigerator. Make the rocket soup up to eight hours ahead. The sauce for the chicken can be prepared up to eight hours in advance, kept covered with clingfilm in the refrigerator, then reheated gently at the last minute. *See pages 88–9 for recipes.*

SUMMER MENU

The garden is a perfect setting for a high summer dinner party. In this menu, the food is light and tantalizingly flavoursome. *Serves 6*

BRIE & LENTIL SALAD
The country flavours of this dish are an immediate transport to sunshine.

TROUT WITH GOOSEBERRY SAUCE
A delicious fish: moist but not oily with a fine, delicate flavour.

STRAWBERRY TART
This tart is most special when made with wild strawberries.

DRINKS
Serve a premier cru Chablis or a Puligny-Montrachet with this menu. If you can find the wild strawberry wine Fragolini, a glass of it would be nectar with the tart.

PLANNING NOTES
The pastry case for the strawberry tart can be made two days in advance and stored in an airtight tin. Prepare the lentils for the salad up to 24 hours ahead. The gooseberry sauce can also be made 24 hours in advance, covered with clingfilm in the refrigerator, and then reheated when required. *See pages 90–1 for recipes.*

GEOFFERY CHAUCER C.1340–1400

VEGETARIAN

A scrumptious mix of flavours in a menu that uses taste and texture to the maximum. *Serves 6*

ROAST TOMATO SOUP
Roasting the tomatoes intensifies their flavour to give an extra fillip to this soup.

BLUE CHEESE SOUFFLÉS
A feather-light, tangy soufflé, juxtaposed with the nutty sweetness of the vegetables.

COFFEE TRUFFLE PUDDING
A dessert with a small surprise at its heart.

DRINKS
A full-bodied Rhône rosé wine such as a Tavel or Lirac will go happily with the soup, and complement the eggs and cheese of the soufflé. A Gewürztraminer would ideally complement the rich dessert.

PLANNING NOTES
The roast tomato soup can be made 24 hours in advance. Don't be daunted by soufflés, these work every time. Just make sure your guests are ready to receive them as they come out of the oven. *See pages 92–3 for recipes.*

FRUITS OF THE SEA

Choose the freshest of ingredients for this delectable dinner. *Serves 6*

PRAWNS IN CIDER
The sweetness of the prawns and the dryness of the cider make them a well-matched pair.

TUNA STEAKS WITH RHUBARB
Rhubarb's sharp taste is a good foil for the robust and oily tuna fish.

MANGO SYLLABUB & ALMOND BISCUITS
An old-fashioned recipe with a distinctive new fruit flavour, delicious served with the biscuits.

DRINKS
Drink cider or a dry apple juice with the prawns. Serve a New World Semillon Chardonnay with the tuna, and a sweet Riesling with the dessert.

PLANNING NOTES
The syllabub can be made up to 24 hours in advance. Bake the biscuits the day before and store in an airtight tin. Cook the prawns up to one hour in advance and keep them hot in the oven. The tuna can also be prepared one hour in advance, and kept covered and just warm in a low oven. *See pages 94–5 for recipes.*

MENUS 3

"Of soup and love the first is the best"

HARVEST SUPPER

Autumn is the perfect time to savour the riches of the harvest at their very freshest. *Serves 6*

WILD MUSHROOM RAGOÛT
A good way to make the most of freshly harvested wild mushrooms gathered in the wild.

PHEASANT & APPLES WITH CALVADOS
The earthy, apple flavour of Calvados gives this traditional Normandy dish its distinctive character.

CHOCOLATE & COFFEE CHEESECAKE
Dark chocolate and coffee make good companions in this wonderful rich cheesecake.

DRINKS
A lightly oaked Chardonnay would have the presence to accompany this meal. Enjoy the dessert with a glass of Madeira.

PLANNING NOTES
The mushroom ragoût can be prepared up to 12 hours in advance, kept covered in the refrigerator, then reheated at the last minute. Cook the pheasant breasts up to two hours ahead of the meal, then keep covered and warm in a low oven. The cheesecake needs at least 8 hours to set, and will last for up to one week in the refrigerator.
See pages 96–7 for recipes.

WINTER DINNER

Serve hearty food to keep the winter cold at bay: a soup scented with saffron, a tender beef stew, and a light, steamed sponge dessert. *Serves 6*

PRAWN, LEEK & SAFFRON SOUP
A melting soup with a great aroma and delicate flavours.

FLEMISH-STYLE BEEF
Cooking beef in beer with herbs lends it a fragrant, tangy-sweet flavour.

STEAMED CRANBERRY PUDDING
This light sponge is topped with a crown of cranberries, and an orange and cranberry sauce.

DRINKS
Follow a white Burgundy with the soup by a mature, smooth, and rich Burgundy Pinot Noir such as a Beaune or Pommard, or a fine Californian Zinfandel. Choose an Australian orange Muscat to round off the meal.

PLANNING NOTES
The beef dish is best cooked up to two days in advance. After cooking (step 4), refrigerate until needed, then reheat in a moderate oven for 30 minutes. The soup can be prepared to the end of step 2, and refrigerated for up to two days. Gently reheat the liquid, and add the prawns and cream. The pudding can be made up to eight hours ahead, then gently reheated in its bowl of simmering water for 15 minutes. Prepare the cranberry sauce in advance, too, then warm just before eating. *See pages 98–9 for recipes.*

ANONYMOUS (SPANISH)

FAMILY GATHERING

It often feels appropriate to serve traditional dishes for family, so here is a menu with soup, roast meat, and a rich dessert. Each course is not quite what you would expect, however! *Serves 12*

ITALIAN CABBAGE SOUP
A hearty soup of cabbage, herbs, and cheese from northern Italy.

SPICY PORK ROAST
Spices, herbs, and rum add a Caribbean touch.

MIRACULOUS BLACKBERRY CAKE
A monster of a dessert with layers of sponge, meringue, cream, and blackberries.

DRINKS
Start with a well-chilled dry sparkling wine such as Proseccodli. Follow it with a good Chianti Classico or Chianti Rufina to match the spicy pork.

PLANNING NOTES
The pork must be marinated for 24 hours. Make the meringue and sponges the day before and store in an airtight tin, but assemble the cake just before your guests arrive, to prevent the cream and berries softening the cake tiers. Layer the soup (to the end of step 4) up to eight hours in advance, then pour on the boiling stock at the last moment and heat through the soup. *See pages 100–1 for recipes.*

COUNTRY FOOD

For an easy and informal meal, serve an interesting pasta followed by vegetable kebabs and a fruit compote. *Serves 6*

ASPARAGUS & HAM FETTUCINE
Ensure that your guests do not eat too much of this delicious pasta as a starter.

VEGETABLE & NUT KEBABS
These kebabs are roasted to perfection with a spicy, piquant peanut sauce.

SPICED QUINCES & EARL GREY SORBET
The quinces, like the tea, are sweetly and delicately perfumed.

DRINKS
Serve a high-quality dry Chenin blanc from South Africa or New Zealand, followed by a lightly sweet Gewürztraminer with the spiced quinces.

PLANNING NOTES
Make the sorbet up to six weeks, and the quinces up to 24 hours, in advance. The vegetables for the pasta will keep for four hours, if covered: cook the pasta, reheat the vegetables, and add them with the cream, cheese, and ham to the pasta at the last moment. Prepare the kebab sauce up to four hours before the meal. The kebabs are best cooked and served in one operation, but the ingredients can be skewered, with a little lemon juice squeezed over them, two hours in advance. *See pages 102–3 for recipes.*

FESTIVE CELEBRATION FOR 6

SEARED PEARS & PARMA HAM

 20 MINUTES   10 MINUTES

INGREDIENTS

3 PEARS (PREFERABLY COMICE)
2 TBSP OLIVE OIL
2 GARLIC CLOVES, SKIN LEFT ON, CRUSHED
UNDER THE FLAT OF A KNIFE
125ML (4FL OZ) BALSAMIC VINEGAR
1 TSP SOFT BROWN SUGAR
18 VERY THIN SLICES OF PARMA HAM OR
PROSCIUTTO
LAMB'S LETTUCE OR WATERCRESS LEAVES TO
SERVE

1 Cut each pear in half and remove the core. Slice each half into 6 wedge-shaped pieces.

2 Heat the olive oil in a frying pan and add the garlic and half of the vinegar. Add the pieces of pear to the pan and brown for about 5 minutes, turning halfway during cooking (the vinegar should become sticky and almost disappear). Remove the pan from the heat. Take out the pears and allow them to cool.

3 Return the pan containing the juices and garlic to the heat and add the sugar and remaining vinegar. Bring to the boil over a high heat. Discard the garlic. Arrange the Parma ham and pears on a bed of lamb's lettuce and drizzle with the hot sauce.

SCALLOPS WITH CHARD

 45 MINUTES   12 MINUTES

INGREDIENTS

12 STEMS OF CHARD
½ LEMON, JUICE ONLY
30 MEDIUM, SHELLED SCALLOPS
100G (3½ OZ) UNSALTED BUTTER
2 GARLIC CLOVES, SKINS LEFT ON, CRUSHED
UNDER THE FLAT OF A KNIFE
90ML (3FL OZ) WHITE VERMOUTH OR DRY
WHITE WINE
SALT & PEPPER TO TASTE

1 Trim the ends of the chard and discard the leaves. Cut the stems into strips and steam for about 10 minutes, until *al dente*. Transfer to a warmed dish, pour over the lemon juice, and keep hot in the oven.

2 While the chard is cooking, rinse the scallops, remove any dark strands, and pat dry with kitchen paper. Detach the corals and purée them in a food processor. Halve the white part of each scallop horizontally to give 2 discs.

3 To make the sauce, heat 75g (2½ oz) of butter in a frying pan. Add the garlic and fry gently until it just begins to brown. Pour in the vermouth, bring to the boil, and simmer for about 5

minutes, until reduced by one-third. Remove from the heat and discard the garlic. Stir in the puréed corals and seasoning. Cover and keep warm.

4 Place the scallops on an oiled baking sheet. Brush with the remaining butter, melted, and sprinkle with salt and pepper on both sides. Place under a high grill and cook for 1 minute each side. Serve on a bed of chard, drizzled with the sauce.

COOK'S TIP
You may have to cook the scallops in 2 batches. Keep them hot in a warmed, covered dish in the oven until ready to serve.

CHOCOLATE TART

🥄 25 MINUTES 🍲 35 MINUTES ▭ 3 HOURS CHILLING

INGREDIENTS

375G (12OZ) SWEET SHORTCRUST PASTRY
(SEE PAGE 184)
375G (12OZ) PLAIN DARK CHOCOLATE
4 TBSP INSTANT COFFEE GRANULES
3 TBSP BRANDY (OPTIONAL)
900ML (1½ PT) DOUBLE CREAM
COCOA POWDER & ICING SUGAR,
SIFTED, TO DECORATE
SINGLE CREAM TO SERVE

COOK'S TIP

This tart is very rich, so serve thin slices. Any leftovers can be kept in an airtight container in the refrigerator for up to 4 days.

1 Roll out the pastry and press into a 25cm (10in) loose-bottomed fluted tart tin. Prick the pastry with a fork then refrigerate for 30 minutes.

2 Preheat oven to 180°C/350°F/Gas 4. Line the dough with greaseproof paper, fill with dried beans, and bake for 15 minutes until the pastry is just set. Remove the greaseproof paper and beans. Return to the oven for a further 15 minutes, until the pastry is crisp and golden. Leave to cool.

3 For the filling, break the chocolate into small pieces, then heat with the coffee in a double boiler, or a heatproof bowl over a pan of simmering water, or microwave, until just melted. Stir gently until smooth, but do not beat. Allow to cool, then stir in the brandy, if using.

4 Whisk the cream until it forms soft peaks then gently fold in the chocolate mixture. Turn into the pastry case. Refrigerate for at least 3 hours.

5 To decorate, remove the tart from the tin and, using 2 strips of cardboard, make a pattern on the surface with cocoa and icing sugar. Serve with single cream.

CHOCOLATE
TART

LAVISH PARTY FOR 12

CRAB TARTLETS WITH LEEK PURÉE

🥄 30 MINUTES 🍲 45 MINUTES

INGREDIENTS

500G (1LB) SHORTCRUST PASTRY (SEE
PAGE 184)
350ML (12FL OZ) CRÈME FRAÎCHE
1 LEMON, GRATED ZEST ONLY
2 EGGS, YOLKS ONLY
375G (12OZ) CRAB MEAT (WHITE & BROWN)
½ TSP GROUND NUTMEG
5 LEEKS (WHITE PART ONLY), FINELY CHOPPED
60G (2OZ) BUTTER
1 TSP SUGAR
1 TBSP DRY SHERRY
GREEN SALAD LEAVES TO SERVE

1 For the crust, roll out the pastry and press into twelve 10cm (4in) round fluted tart tins. Prick the bottom of the pastry cases all over with a fork then refrigerate for 30 minutes.

2 Preheat oven to 200°C/400°F/Gas 6. Line the dough with greaseproof paper, fill with dried beans, and bake for 15 minutes. Remove the grease-proof paper and beans. Leave to cool.

3 To make the filling, beat the crème fraîche, lemon zest, and egg yolks in a mixing bowl until well mixed, then stir in the crab meat.

4 Spoon the filling into the pastry cases and sprinkle a pinch of nutmeg over each tartlet. Bake for a further 15 minutes until golden.

5 To make the purée, place the leeks in a saucepan with the butter, sugar, and sherry, bring to boil, cover, and simmer for 10 minutes until soft, then blend in a food processor. Serve the tartlets warm with 2 tablespoons of warm purée per person and a garnish of green salad leaves.

CRAB TARTLETS WITH
LEEK PURÉE

DUCK WITH KUMQUATS
30 MINUTES · 35 MINUTES

INGREDIENTS
8 DUCK BREASTS, SKINS LEFT ON
2 TSP CASTER SUGAR
2 TBSP OLIVE OIL
2 GARLIC CLOVES, SKINS LEFT ON, CRUSHED
UNDER THE FLAT OF A KNIFE
325G (11 OZ) KUMQUATS
125ML (4FL OZ) ORANGE LIQUEUR
(PREFERABLY COINTREAU) OR 2 TBSP HONEY
575ML (18FL OZ) RED WINE
575ML (18FL OZ) ORANGE JUICE
HERBY POTATOES (SEE PAGE 186) & ROAST
SHALLOTS (SEE PAGE 187) TO SERVE

1 Preheat oven to 200°C/400°F/Gas 6. Make diagonal slits in the skin of the duck breasts to create a lattice effect. Sprinkle the sugar on both sides.

2 Heat the olive oil in a large frying pan over a high heat. Add the garlic, then 4 of the duck breasts, skin side down. Cook for 3 minutes on each side until they are rich brown, almost burnt. Repeat with the remaining duck breasts, reserving the cooking juices and oil for the sauce in the pan.

3 Place all the breasts on a rack over a foil-lined roasting tin and bake in the oven for 18 minutes (the duck should remain pink inside).

4 Meanwhile, make the sauce. Slice each kumquat into 4 rounds and remove the pips. Remove all but 2 tablespoons of the fat from the frying pan, and reserve the browned bits and garlic cloves. Return the pan to a moderate heat.

5 Add the kumquats to the pan. Pour in the orange liqueur and carefully set light to it (if using honey, do not flambé). When the flames have died, stir in the wine, scraping all the browned bits from the sides of the pan. Bring to the boil and reduce the liquid to about 4 tablespoons. Add the orange juice and reduce by half, stirring occasionally. Discard the garlic.

6 Slice each duck breast, and apportion between the plates, allowing three-quarters of a breast per person. Pour over the sauce, and serve with Herby Potatoes, Roast Shallots, and a green leaf salad.

COOK'S TIP
If cooking for six, use four breasts, and halve the remaining ingredients.

SUMMER FRUITS WITH CRÈME FRAÎCHE
10 MINUTES · 5 MINUTES

INGREDIENTS
275G (9OZ) STRAWBERRIES (PREFERABLY
WILD)
275G (9OZ) RASPBERRIES
275G (9OZ) CHERRIES, PITTED
500ML (17FL OZ) CRÈME FRAÎCHE
3 EGGS, YOLKS ONLY
125G (4OZ) CASTER SUGAR
3 TBSP ROSE WATER

1 Combine the strawberries, raspberries, and cherries and spread them over the base of a large, shallow ovenproof dish.

2 Preheat the grill to high. In a large mixing bowl, whisk together the crème fraîche, egg yolks, 90g (3oz) of caster sugar, and the rose water until completely smooth. Pour the cream mixture over the fruits.

3 Sprinkle the remaining sugar over the surface and place the dish under the grill for about 5 minutes, until the top just begins to brown. Serve immediately.

COOK'S TIP
Make certain that you use a heat-resistant dish as the grill must be extremely hot.

INTIMATE DINNER FOR 2

HERB OMELETTE WITH CAVIAR

—— 10 MINUTES 8 MINUTES ——

INGREDIENTS
4 LARGE EGGS, SEPARATED
4 TBSP FRESH PARSLEY, FINELY CHOPPED, PLUS
SPRIGS TO GARNISH
2 TBSP DOUBLE CREAM
SALT & PEPPER TO TASTE
30G (1OZ) BUTTER
1 TBSP OLIVE OIL
2 TBSP CAVIAR OR LUMPFISH ROE

1 Mix the egg yolks with the chopped parsley, cream, and seasoning.

2 In a mixing bowl, whisk the egg whites until they form stiff peaks. Fold the egg yolk mixture into the whites.

3 Turn the grill to high. Divide the butter and oil between two 20cm (8in) frying pans and heat until the butter just begins to brown. Add half of the egg mixture to each pan and turn the heat to low. Cook for 4 minutes.

4 Place the omelettes in their pans under the grill and cook for 3–4 minutes until golden and risen.

5 Place one tablespoon of caviar in the centre of each omelette, spread along the centre and fold in half. Garnish with the parsley sprigs and serve immediately.

COOK'S TIP
This dish must be cooked and eaten immediately, so make sure you and your guest are ready.

LOBSTER WITH ROAST FIGS

—— 15 MINUTES 25 MINUTES ——

INGREDIENTS
4 FIGS
175G (6OZ) UNSALTED BUTTER, CHILLED
& IN PIECES
2 TSP BALSAMIC VINEGAR
2 X 750G (1½LB) LIVE LOBSTERS
3 TBSP OLIVE OIL
2 TBSP SHERRY VINEGAR
2 TBSP WATER
1 SHALLOT, FINELY CHOPPED
1 TBSP FRESH DILL, FINELY CHOPPED
SALT & PEPPER TO TASTE
GREEN SALAD LEAVES & WALNUT DRESSING
(SEE PAGE 185) TO SERVE

COOK'S TIP
To cut the lobsters open, use a very sharp, serrated knife. Remove and discard the dark, thread-like membrane that runs down the length of the lobster before serving.

1 Preheat oven to 230°C/450°F/Gas 8. Remove the tips of the figs, and make 2 cuts at right angles to about three-quarters of the way down. Ease them open and place 1 teaspoon of butter and ½ teaspoon of balsamic vinegar into the centres. Set aside.

2 Next, plunge the lobsters into a large saucepan of boiling water, then immediately remove them. Brush all over with oil, then place them in a roasting tin in the oven.

3 After 8 minutes of cooking, add the figs to the roasting tin containing the lobsters. Bake for a further 10 minutes. While the lobsters and figs are cooking, make the sauce.

4 Heat the sherry vinegar, water, shallot, dill, and seasoning in a small saucepan. Cook gently for 5 minutes, until the shallot has softened and the liquid has almost disappeared.

5 Over a low to medium heat, beat in the remaining butter, one piece at a time, whisking between each addition until all the butter has been used and the sauce is rich and creamy. Pour it into a sauce boat, cover with clingfilm, and keep warm.

6 Cut the lobsters in half lengthways and discard the heads. Arrange the bodies and claws on a bed of salad with Walnut Dressing. Serve with the roast figs and lastly, pour on the sauce.

LOBSTER
WITH
ROAST FIGS

ORANGE & GRAPEFRUIT SORBETS

🥄 25 MINUTES   🍲 20 MINUTES   ⬜ 8 HOURS CHILLING

INGREDIENTS
600ML (1PT) WATER
625G (1¼LB) SUGAR
12 BLOOD ORANGES, JUICE ONLY, CHILLED
2 TSP ANGOSTURA BITTERS
2 LARGE EGGS, WHITES ONLY
3 PINK GRAPEFRUIT, JUICE ONLY, CHILLED
2 TBSP OUZO
FRESH MINT LEAVES TO DECORATE

1 For the orange sorbet, heat half each of the water and sugar in a saucepan. Bring to the boil, stirring until the sugar has dissolved. Add the orange juice and bitters.

2 Make the grapefruit sorbet in the same way, using grapefruit juice and ouzo instead of orange juice and bitters. Leave both mixtures to cool, then refrigerate for at least 2 hours, until thoroughly chilled.

3 Pour the mixtures into two rigid freezerproof containers, cover, and freeze for 3 hours, stirring both at the end of each hour. On the final stirring, lightly beat the egg whites and stir them into the sorbet. Return to the freezer for at least 3 hours.

4 Transfer 2 scoops of each sorbet per person to the refrigerator 30 minutes before serving to soften. Serve decorated with fresh mint leaves.

EXOTIC EVENING FOR 6

PEPPERED SCALLOPS

 35 MINUTES ⊓ 35 MINUTES

INGREDIENTS

475ML (16FL OZ) WHIPPING CREAM
½ YELLOW PEPPER, THINLY SLICED
½ RED PEPPER, THINLY SLICED
1 TBSP PAPRIKA
½ LEMON, JUICE & GRATED ZEST
SALT TO TASTE
18 LARGE SHELLED SCALLOPS
2 TBSP MILD WHOLEGRAIN MUSTARD
3 TBSP PINK PEPPERCORNS, CRUSHED
30G (1OZ) UNSALTED BUTTER
2 TBSP OLIVE OIL
GREEN SALAD LEAVES & SAFFRON RICE
(SEE PAGE 187) TO SERVE

COOK'S TIP

Scallops are a great delicacy, ideal for an intimate gathering, but bear in mind that they are very costly if you are entertaining on a larger scale.

1 To make the sauces, divide the cream between 2 small saucepans. Add the yellow pepper to one, the red pepper and paprika to the other.

2 Bring them to the boil, cover, then simmer gently for 15 minutes. Allow to cool. Stir the lemon juice and zest into the yellow pepper mixture,

then liquidize each sauce separately in a blender until smooth. Season to taste.

3 Remove and discard the corals and any dark strands from the scallops. Pat dry with kitchen paper. Coat them in mustard, then dip them in the crushed peppercorns.

4 In a large frying pan, heat the butter and olive oil until the butter just begins to brown. Sauté the scallops in a single layer for about 3 minutes, turning halfway through cooking, until golden and just cooked.

5 Serve immediately, on a bed of green salad leaves, with Saffron Rice and 2 tablespoons of each sauce per person.

LAMB TAGINE
WITH
COUSCOUS

LAMB TAGINE WITH COUSCOUS

 30 MINUTES · 1 HOUR 20 MINUTES

INGREDIENTS

1.75KG (3½ LB) BONED SHOULDER OF LAMB
3 TBSP OLIVE OIL
3 ONIONS, FINELY CHOPPED
3 GARLIC CLOVES, CRUSHED
60G (2OZ) FRESH WHITE BREADCRUMBS
2 FRESH PLUM TOMATOES, SKINNED & CHOPPED
4 TBSP FRESH CORIANDER, FINELY CHOPPED
6 TBSP FRESH PARSLEY, FINELY CHOPPED
2 TSP EACH GROUND CORIANDER,
GINGER, & CUMIN
1 TSP EACH OF GROUND CLOVES & CINNAMON
1 TBSP SOFT BROWN SUGAR
1 LEMON, JUICE & GRATED ZEST
125G (4OZ) PRUNES, PITTED &
COARSELY CHOPPED
250ML (8FL OZ) DRY WHITE WINE
600ML (1PT) VEGETABLE STOCK
(SEE PAGE 185)
SALT & PEPPER TO TASTE
COUSCOUS (SEE PAGE 187) TO SERVE

1 Preheat oven to 180°C/350°F/Gas 4. Trim the lamb of excess fat, keeping the skin on.

2 Next, make the stuffing. Heat 2 tablespoons of oil in a frying pan over a low heat, add two-thirds of the onion and two-thirds of the garlic, cover, and cook gently for 5 minutes, until softened.

3 In a large bowl, combine the breadcrumbs, tomatoes, all the herbs and spices, sugar, lemon juice and zest, and prunes. Add the garlic and onions.

4 Place the lamb skin-side down, and spread stuffing mixture over the upper surface. Roll up tightly to form a cylinder with the skin on the outside, and tie securely with string. Insert small skewers through the ends of the roll to seal it.

5 Heat the remaining oil in the frying pan and brown the lamb for about 5 minutes all over. Transfer to an oiled roasting tin and cook in the middle of the oven for 1 hour 15 minutes.

6 While the meat is cooking, make the sauce. To the frying pan, add the remaining onions and garlic. Pour in the wine and stock and scrape up the browned bits. Cook, covered, over a low heat for 45 minutes, until reduced to 300ml (½ pint). Adjust seasoning and strain into a sauce boat.

7 Leave the meat to stand for 15 minutes before carving, then serve with the sauce, Couscous, and mangetouts.

COOK'S TIP
If the outside of the lamb appears to be turning brown too quickly, cover it with aluminium foil.

COCONUT & SAFFRON ICE CREAM

20 MINUTES · 15 MINUTES · 8 HOURS CHILLING

INGREDIENTS

350ML (12FL OZ) COCONUT MILK
150G (5OZ) CASTER SUGAR
½ TSP GROUND SAFFRON
4 EGGS, YOLKS ONLY
500ML (17FL OZ) SINGLE CREAM, CHILLED
½ TSP SAFFRON THREADS, CRUSHED
100G (3½ OZ) FRESH GRATED OR SHREDDED
COCONUT, LIGHTLY TOASTED, & CHILLED

COOK'S TIP
If you have an ice cream maker, follow the instructions given, adding the coconut for the last 6 minutes.

1 Heat the coconut milk, sugar, and ground saffron in a pan, stirring to dissolve the sugar. As soon as the mixture comes to the boil, pour it over the egg yolks, whisking constantly.

2 Pour the mixture into a double boiler, or heatproof bowl over a pan of simmering water, stirring all the time. As soon as it coats the back of a spoon (after about 5 minutes), remove from the heat. Do not allow to boil. Leave to cool, then refrigerate for at least 2 hours, until thoroughly chilled.

3 Whisk in the chilled single cream and the saffron threads.

4 Pour the mixture into a rigid freezerproof container, cover, and freeze for 3 hours, stirring at the end of each hour. On the final stirring, fold in the grated coconut. Refreeze for at least 3 hours. Transfer to the refrigerator 30 minutes before serving to soften.

SPRING DINNER FOR 6

ROCKET SOUP

 20 MINUTES · 40 MINUTES

INGREDIENTS

1 TBSP SUNFLOWER OIL
1 ONION, COARSELY CHOPPED
100G (3½ OZ) BUTTER
3 TBSP PLAIN FLOUR
1.5 LITRES (2½ PT) CHICKEN OR VEGETABLE STOCK (SEE PAGE 185)
2 TSP GREEN PEPPERCORNS, GROUND
SALT TO TASTE
300G (10OZ) ROCKET LEAVES
2 EGGS, YOLKS ONLY
RAISIN & OREGANO SODA BREAD (SEE PAGE 160) TO SERVE

1 Heat the oil in a large saucepan and fry the onion until softened. Mix half of the butter with the flour to form a paste, then add to the onion over a moderate heat, stirring all the time, until the flour is just cooked, but not brown (about 5 minutes).

2 Add the stock, a little at a time, stirring thoroughly between each addition. When it has all been added, sprinkle in the pepper and salt, cover, and simmer for approximately 30 minutes, stirring occasionally.

3 Meanwhile, cook the rocket in a large saucepan of salted boiling water for 3 minutes and drain.

4 In a blender, liquidize the rocket with the egg yolks and the remaining butter until smooth, then add a ladleful of stock and mix. Pour back into the stock and cook, stirring until thickened. Do not boil. Serve hot with Raisin and Oregano Soda Bread.

COOK'S TIP
On a warm summer's evening, this soup is delicious served chilled.

TARRAGON CHICKEN

20 MINUTES · 25 MINUTES

INGREDIENTS

4 SHALLOTS, FINELY CHOPPED
3 TBSP WHITE WINE VINEGAR
1 LEMON, JUICE & GRATED ZEST
3 TBSP DRY WHITE WINE
325ML (11FL OZ) CHICKEN STOCK (SEE PAGE 185)
1 TBSP GREEN PEPPERCORNS, CRUSHED
1 BAY LEAF
2 TSP FRESH TARRAGON, FINELY CHOPPED
2 TBSP CRÈME FRAÎCHE
2 TBSP SUNFLOWER OIL
6 CHICKEN BREASTS, BONED & SKINNED
SALT TO TASTE
125ML (4FL OZ) TARRAGON OR HONEY MUSTARD
150G (5OZ) FRESH WHITE BREADCRUMBS
BABY NEW POTATOES & MANGETOUTS TO SERVE

1 For the sauce, put the shallots in a saucepan with the vinegar, lemon juice and zest, and wine. Bring to the boil, then simmer gently for about 5 minutes, until the shallots are softened and the liquid has almost disappeared.

2 Add the stock, peppercorns, bay leaf, and tarragon, and simmer for a further 7 minutes, then add the crème fraîche, mixing thoroughly. Strain the sauce into a sauce boat and keep warm.

3 Preheat grill to medium. Line a roasting tin with foil and place a wire rack inside it. Brush oil over both sides of the chicken, season with a little salt, then grill on the wire rack for 3–5 minutes on each side.

4 Remove the roasting tin from the heat and coat both sides of the chicken breasts with the mustard, then gently roll them in the breadcrumbs.

5 Dab the chicken with oil from the roasting tin and return to the grill to cook for a further 5 minutes each side, until the chicken is golden and cooked through. Pour over the sauce and serve with baby new potatoes and mangetouts.

COOK'S TIP
This dish is also excellent made with guinea fowl, pheasant, or turkey breasts.

LIME & MINT MOULD

1 HOUR ✓ 5 MINUTES ⏢ 3 HOURS CHILLING

INGREDIENTS

375ML (13FL OZ) SWEET WHITE WINE
3 LIMES, JUICE OF 3 & GRATED ZEST OF 2
3 TBSP CASTER SUGAR
2 TBSP FRESH MINT, FINELY CHOPPED, PLUS
WHOLE MINT LEAVES TO DECORATE
2 TBSP POWDERED GELATINE
600ML (1PT) SINGLE CREAM
175G (6OZ) RASPBERRIES OR OTHER SOFT
FRUITS
2 TBSP ICING SUGAR, SIFTED

COOK'S TIPS

Use vegetarian gelatine if you prefer.
Leaf gelatine can also be used instead
of the powdered type; 30g (1oz) will
set this mould, or follow the
instructions on the packet.

LIME & MINT
MOULD

1 To make the jelly, heat the wine (reserve 4 tablespoons for the gelatine), juice and zest of 2 limes, caster sugar, and mint in a saucepan. Bring almost to the boil, then remove from the heat.

2 In a small saucepan, sprinkle the gelatine over the reserved wine. Leave to soak for 5 minutes. Place over a very low heat and stir until dissolved. Stir into the warmed wine mixture.

3 When the mixture has cooled to room temperature, add the cream and stir well. Pour the mixture into an oiled 1.25 litre (2 pint) mould. Chill for at least 3 hours (but not more than 48).

4 For the sauce, roughly mash the fruits, reserving a few whole pieces for decoration, then add the juice of 1 lime and the icing sugar, and mix well. Pass the mixture through a fine sieve.

5 Gently warm the mould to help loosen the jelly by immersing it to the rim in warm water. Invert the jelly onto a serving plate. Spoon the sauce around the jelly and decorate with whole fruits and mint leaves.

SUMMER MENU FOR 6

BRIE & LENTIL SALAD

15 MINUTES 30 MINUTES

INGREDIENTS

1 TBSP VEGETABLE OIL
3 ONIONS, FINELY CHOPPED
2 GARLIC CLOVES, CRUSHED
250G (8OZ) LENTILS (PREFERABLY PUY)
1 LEMON, JUICE ONLY
600ML (1PT) WATER
4 SPRIGS FRESH THYME, PLUS 6 TO GARNISH
1 BAY LEAF
SALT & PEPPER TO TASTE
125ML (4FL OZ) HAZELNUT DRESSING
(SEE PAGE 185)
375G (12OZ) RIPE BRIE, THINLY SLICED
GREEN HERB LEAVES TO GARNISH

COOK'S TIP

Green or orange lentils need less time to cook: follow the manufacturer's instructions if you use them.

1 Heat the oil in a saucepan, add the onions and garlic and fry gently for about 5 minutes, until softened. Stir in the lentils, then pour on the lemon juice and water.

2 Add the thyme, bay leaf, and seasoning to the pan, bring to the boil then simmer for approximately 20 minutes, until the lentils are *al dente* and the water has been absorbed.

Discard the thyme and bay leaf and drain the lentils thoroughly.

3 Return the lentils to the pan and stir in 4 tablespoons of Hazelnut Dressing. Leave to cool until the mixture reaches room temperature.

4 For each portion, fill a 5cm (2in) ring mould with the lentil mixture. Press down well and invert it carefully onto a plate. Arrange a few slices of brie and green herb leaves on the same plate. Drizzle with the Hazelnut Dressing and season the brie with freshly ground black pepper. Garnish each portion of lentils with a sprig of thyme.

BRIE & LENTIL SALAD

TROUT WITH GOOSEBERRY SAUCE

🥄 25 MINUTES 🍲 15 MINUTES

INGREDIENTS

250G (8OZ) GOOSEBERRIES
1½ TBSP SUGAR
4 TBSP WATER
175G (6OZ) BUTTER
½ TSP GROUND GINGER
6 TROUT (PREFERABLY RIVER OR BROWN),
FILLETED, CLEANED, FINS & GILLS TRIMMED,
HEADS LEFT ON
PLAIN FLOUR TO DUST
SALT & PEPPER TO TASTE
4 TBSP OLIVE OIL
NEW POTATOES & SALAD LEAVES TO SERVE
FLAT-LEAF PARSLEY TO GARNISH

1 To make the sauce, place the gooseberries, sugar, and water in a saucepan and simmer gently for 5 minutes, stirring occasionally until soft. Drain thoroughly.

2 Return the mix to the saucepan, beat in one-third of the butter and the ginger to form a purée. Pour into a sauce boat and keep warm.

3 Dust the trout on each side with seasoned flour. In a large frying pan, heat the olive oil with the remaining butter. Over a moderate heat, cook each trout for 4 minutes on each side, until golden.

4 Place 1 trout on each plate, pour over the gooseberry sauce, and garnish with flat-leaf parsley. Serve with new potatoes and a green salad.

COOK'S TIPS

If gooseberries are unavailable, use peeled, cored, roughly chopped cooking apples, with an extra tablespoon of water, or use 250g (8oz) rhubarb. Cook the trout in 2 batches if necessary, keeping the prepared ones warm, covered, in the oven.

STRAWBERRY TART

🥄 20 MINUTES 🍲 25 MINUTES

INGREDIENTS

375G (12OZ) SWEET SHORTCRUST PASTRY
(SEE PAGE 184)
400ML (14FL OZ) DOUBLE CREAM
400ML (14FL OZ) FROMAGE FRAIS
3 TBSP ICING SUGAR SIFTED, PLUS
EXTRA TO DUST
1 TBSP ROSE WATER
500G (1LB) STRAWBERRIES (PREFERABLY WILD)
4 TBSP REDCURRANT JELLY, MELTED

COOK'S TIPS

Raspberries can also be used instead of strawberries. The pastry case can be made two days in advance and kept in an airtight tin.

1 For the crust, roll out the pastry and press into a 25cm (10in) loose-bottomed fluted tart tin. Prick the bottom of the pastry all over with a fork, then refrigerate for 30 minutes to prevent it shrinking when baked.

2 Preheat oven to 180°C/350°F/Gas 4. Line the dough with greaseproof paper, fill with dried beans, and bake for 15 minutes, until the pastry is just set. Remove the beans and greaseproof paper. Return to the oven for a further 15 minutes, until the pastry is crisp and golden. Leave to cool.

3 To make the filling, beat the cream, fromage frais, icing sugar, and rose water until thick and spread over the pastry base. Arrange the strawberries on top in the pastry case.

4 Brush the strawberries with the cooled redcurrant jelly to glaze. Dust the edge of the pastry case with icing sugar and serve.

VEGETARIAN FOR 6

ROAST TOMATO SOUP

15 MINUTES · 1 HOUR 35 MINUTES

INGREDIENTS
2KG (4LB) FRESH PLUM TOMATOES
5 TBSP OLIVE OIL
1 TBSP EACH FENNEL & CUMIN SEEDS
2 ONIONS, COARSELY CHOPPED
2 FRESH GREEN CHILLIES, DESEEDED & FINELY CHOPPED
4 GARLIC CLOVES, COARSELY CHOPPED
4 KAFFIR LIME LEAVES
2 LIMES, JUICE & GRATED ZEST
1 TBSP SOFT BROWN SUGAR
600ML (1PT) WATER
2 TBSP TOMATO PURÉE
5 TBSP FRESH BASIL, COARSELY CHOPPED
SALT & PEPPER TO TASTE
SOURED CREAM TO SERVE

1 Preheat oven to 200°C/400°F/Gas 6. Slice the tomatoes in half, brush with 3 tablespoons of the olive oil, and place cut face up on a lined baking sheet. Roast for 1 hour.

2 Meanwhile, in a heavy frying pan, dry roast the fennel and cumin for about 3 minutes, until fragrant. Leave to cool, then grind using a pestle and mortar or an electric grinder.

3 Heat the remaining oil. Gently fry the onions, chillies, and garlic for about 8 minutes, until they are softened and just beginning to brown.

4 When the tomatoes are roasted, combine all the ingredients, except the basil and sour cream, in a large saucepan. Bring to the boil and simmer gently for 20 minutes.

5 Discard the kaffir lime leaves. Adjust the seasoning to taste. Liquidize the soup in a blender with the fresh basil until smooth. Serve with a swirl of sour cream.

COOK'S TIPS
Use other tomatoes if plum are not available. If you cannot find kaffir lime leaves (Oriental stores stock them), use the grated zest of 2 limes.

BLUE CHEESE SOUFFLÉS

15 MINUTES · 20 MINUTES

INGREDIENTS
100G (3½ OZ) STILTON (OR OTHER HARD BLUE-VEINED CHEESE)
4 TBSP FRESH BASIL, COARSELY CHOPPED
100G (3½ OZ) BUTTER
75G (2½ OZ) PLAIN FLOUR, SIFTED
SALT TO TASTE
500ML (17FL OZ) MILK
6 LARGE EGGS, SEPARATED: 6 WHITES, 4 YOLKS
STEAMED CHARD & ASPARAGUS TO SERVE

COOK'S TIPS
This recipe is not suitable for more than 6, as the soufflés need to be eaten immediately. Placing the baking sheet in the preheating oven to warm helps the soufflés to rise.

1 Preheat oven to 180°C/350°F/Gas 4. Place the Stilton and basil in a food processor and work until it is the consistency of coarse breadcrumbs.

2 Heat the butter in a saucepan. Mix together the flour, salt, and milk, and gradually add to the butter, stirring constantly. Cook over a very low heat for 5 minutes, stirring constantly, until thickened and smooth. Remove from the heat and stir in the cheese mixture. Leave to cool slightly.

3 Whisk the egg whites with a pinch of salt until they form stiff peaks.

4 Place the cheese sauce into a large mixing bowl. Add the 4 egg yolks and beat lightly until well mixed. Carefully fold in one-quarter of the egg whites, then add the remainder until just combined.

5 Spoon the mixture into 12 greased 7cm (3in) ramekins or soufflé dishes; do not fill more than two-thirds full. Place on a warmed baking sheet and bake for about 15 minutes, or until the tops are just set. Serve immediately with steamed chard and asparagus.

COFFEE TRUFFLE PUDDINGS

🥄 15 MINUTES 🍲 20 MINUTES

INGREDIENTS

125G (4OZ) UNSALTED BUTTER, SOFTENED
150G (5OZ) CASTER SUGAR
4 TSP INSTANT COFFEE GRANULES, DISSOLVED IN
1 TBSP HOT WATER
2 LARGE EGGS
125G (4OZ) PLAIN FLOUR, SIFTED
1 TSP BAKING POWDER, SIFTED
6 PLAIN DARK CHOCOLATE TRUFFLES
125G (4FL OZ) SINGLE CREAM
1 TSP VANILLA EXTRACT

COOK'S TIP

Rum truffles are particularly good, as is a teaspoon of rum added to the cream sauce.

1 Preheat oven to 190°C/375°F/Gas 5. Cream the butter, 125g (4oz) of the caster sugar, and coffee until fluffy. Gradually add the eggs until they are well combined. Do not overbeat. Fold in the flour and baking powder.

2 Grease 6 x 6cm (2½in) ramekins. Place 1 heaped tablespoon of mixture into each ramekin, then lay a truffle on top. Spoon over more mixture, ensuring that it completely surrounds the truffle, until the ramekins are three-quarters full. Bake

for 15–18 minutes, until the puddings are springy to the touch.

3 Meanwhile, make the sauce. Gently heat the cream, remaining caster sugar, and vanilla in a saucepan. Stir until the sugar has dissolved.

4 Remove the ramekins from the oven and leave for 5 minutes before turning out onto individual plates. Serve warm surrounded by the creamy sauce.

BLUE CHEESE
SOUFFLÉS

FRUITS OF THE SEA FOR 6

PRAWNS IN CIDER

— 25 MINUTES   8 MINUTES —

INGREDIENTS
30 RAW TIGER PRAWNS, ABOUT 500G (1LB)
2 TBSP SUNFLOWER OIL
2 GARLIC CLOVES, SKINS LEFT ON, CRUSHED
UNDER THE FLAT OF A KNIFE
4 TBSP CALVADOS OR BRANDY
250ML (8FL OZ) STRONG DRY CIDER
BREAD & BUTTER TO SERVE
GREEN SALAD LEAVES TO GARNISH

1 To prepare the prawns, break or cut off the head and peel off the shell, leaving the tail on. With a small, sharp knife, make a shallow cut along the centre back; remove the dark intestinal vein. Pat dry with kitchen paper.

2 Heat the oil in a frying pan until very hot then add the garlic and the prawns and cook for about 1 minute each side, until they turn pink. Transfer to a warmed dish to keep hot in the oven.

3 Add the Calvados to the pan and carefully set light to it. When the flames have died, add the cider. Boil until the liquid has almost gone.

4 Discard the garlic. Return the prawns to the pan, stirring, to coat them in the sauce. Serve with bread and butter and salad leaves to garnish.

COOK'S TIP
Drink cider as an excellent accompaniment to this delicious northern French starter.

TUNA STEAKS WITH RHUBARB

— 20 MINUTES   15 MINUTES —

INGREDIENTS
1KG (2LB) TUNA STEAK
SALT & PEPPER TO TASTE
6 TBSP OLIVE OIL
300ML (½ PT) PORT OR MEDIUM DRY SHERRY
3 TBSP BALSAMIC VINEGAR
250G (8OZ) RHUBARB, STALKS ONLY, CUT
INTO 1CM (½ IN) PIECES
1 TBSP FISH SAUCE
300ML (½ PT) VEGETABLE STOCK
(SEE PAGE 185)
CASTER SUGAR TO TASTE
½ ORANGE, JUICE & GRATED ZEST
GREEN SALAD & HERB LEAVES TO SERVE

1 Rub the seasoning into the tuna. Heat 1 tablespoon of oil in a large frying pan over a high heat. When the oil is hot, sear the tuna all over.

2 Turn the heat to medium and cook for a further 6 minutes, turning occasionally. Transfer to a warmed dish, covered, to keep hot in the oven.

3 To make the sauce, pour the port and 2 tablespoons of vinegar into the pan, scraping any remaining browned bits of tuna, and stir. Cook over a moderate heat until the liquid is reduced by half. Add the rhubarb, fish sauce, and stock, and again reduce by half. Taste and add a pinch of caster sugar if necessary.

4 To make the dressing, combine the remaining vinegar, the remaining oil, the orange juice and zest. Mix well, and season if necessary.

5 Carve the tuna into slices, approximately 5mm (¼ in) thick (the fish should be very rare). To serve, put a few mixed salad and herb leaves on each plate and spoon over the orange dressing. Arrange the tuna slices on the same plate and pour over the rhubarb sauce.

COOK'S TIP
Tuna is best served rare, but you should check with your guests first in case anyone would prefer a slightly more cooked steak.

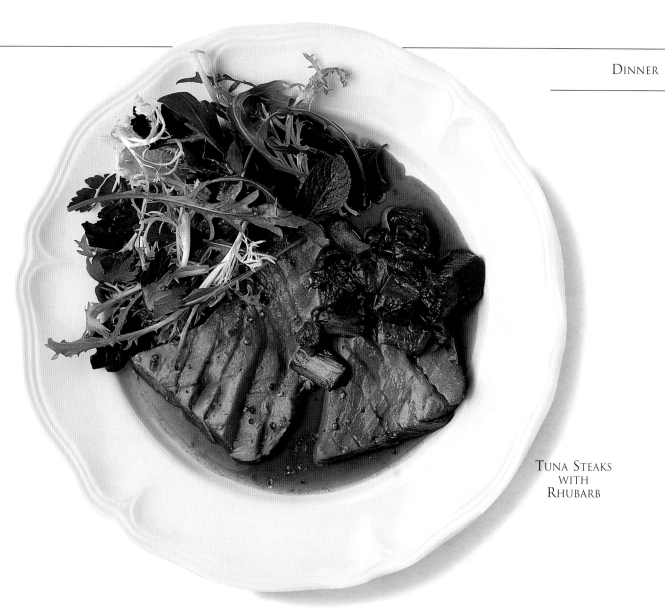

TUNA STEAKS
WITH
RHUBARB

MANGO SYLLABUB & ALMOND BISCUITS

🥄 40 MINUTES   🍲 6 MINUTES

INGREDIENTS

3 RIPE MANGOES, PEELED, STONE REMOVED &
COARSELY CHOPPED

3 TBSP CASTER SUGAR

1 LIME, JUICE & GRATED ZEST

150ML (¼ PT) MANGO JUICE

4 TBSP KIRSCH

450ML (¾ PT) DOUBLE CREAM

90G (3OZ) PLAIN FLOUR, SIFTED

175G (6OZ) ICING SUGAR, SIFTED

175G (6OZ) FLAKED ALMONDS

90ML (3FL OZ) ORANGE JUICE

2 DROPS ALMOND EXTRACT

125G (4OZ) UNSALTED BUTTER, MELTED

1 To make the syllabub, add the mango to the caster sugar, lime juice and zest, mango juice, and Kirsch. Blend in a food processor until smooth.

2 Whisk the cream until it just begins to thicken, then beat in the mango mixture until the cream holds its shape. Spoon into wine glasses or individual dishes and chill until needed.

3 To make the almond biscuits, preheat oven to 200°C/400°F/Gas 6. Mix the flour, icing sugar, and almonds in a large bowl. Add the orange juice, almond essence, and butter. Mix well.

4 Line a baking sheet with baking parchment and place about 30 heaped teaspoons of the mixture roughly 10cm (4in) apart. Smooth down the mixture to make rounds.

5 Bake for 6 minutes or until golden. Leave on the baking sheet for 1 minute, then transfer to a wire rack to cool. Serve the biscuits with the mango syllabub.

COOK'S TIP

For curved biscuits, wrap them around a rolling pin to shape while they are still hot.

HARVEST SUPPER FOR 6

WILD MUSHROOM RAGOÛT

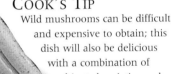 15 MINUTES 15 MINUTES

INGREDIENTS
1KG (2LB) WILD MUSHROOMS
SALT TO TASTE
2 TBSP OLIVE OIL
2 GARLIC CLOVES, SKINS LEFT ON, CRUSHED
UNDER THE FLAT OF A KNIFE
250ML (8FL OZ) RED VERMOUTH, MEDIUM
DRY SHERRY, OR SWEET WHITE WINE
1 TBSP GROUND CORIANDER
½ TSP GROUND NUTMEG
2 SPRIGS FRESH TARRAGON
FRESH CORIANDER, FINELY CHOPPED,
TO GARNISH

1 To prepare the mushrooms, scrape away the dirt with a sharp knife and wipe clean with kitchen paper. Never leave wild mushrooms to soak in water. Cut the mushrooms into bite-sized pieces, discarding the stalks, and sprinkle with salt.

2 Heat the oil in a large frying pan, and gently fry the mushrooms with the garlic over a high heat for about 8 minutes, stirring constantly, until the mushrooms are almost cooked.

3 Add the vermouth, ground coriander, nutmeg, and tarragon, and cook rapidly for approximately 5 minutes, until the vermouth has reduced to about 6 tablespoons. Discard the garlic and tarragon sprigs. Garnish with fresh coriander and serve with garlic bread or lightly toasted brioche sprinkled with sea salt.

COOK'S TIP
Wild mushrooms can be difficult and expensive to obtain; this dish will also be delicious with a combination of cultivated varieties such as field, button, horse, and chestnut mushrooms.

WILD
MUSHROOM
RAGOÛT

PHEASANT & APPLES WITH CALVADOS

🥄 20 MINUTES 🍲 20 MINUTES

INGREDIENTS

4 GREEN EATING APPLES (PREFERABLY GRANNY SMITHS)
1 LEMON, JUICE ONLY
60G (2OZ) BUTTER
4 TBSP OLIVE OIL
6 PHEASANT BREASTS, BONED & SKINNED
2 TSP SUGAR
SALT & PEPPER TO TASTE
4 TBSP CALVADOS OR BRANDY
250ML (8FL OZ) DRY WHITE WINE
4 TBSP CRÈME FRAÎCHE
SPINACH & HERBY POTATOES (SEE PAGE 186) TO SERVE

1 Cut the apples into quarters and remove the cores, then cut each quarter into 4 slices. Shake them in a bowl with half of the lemon juice.

2 In a large frying pan, heat half each of the butter and olive oil, and gently fry the apples for 3 minutes, until golden. Transfer to a warmed ovenproof dish to keep hot.

3 In the same pan, heat the rest of the butter and olive oil. Add the pheasant, sprinkle with the sugar and the remaining lemon juice, season, and cook until pale golden on both sides. Turn heat to low, cover, and cook for 4–5 minutes on each side. Transfer to the ovenproof dish to keep hot.

4 To make the sauce, turn heat to medium, and heat the Calvados in the same pan. Scrape the browned bits around the sides and stir. Almost immediately set light to the alcohol.

5 When the flames have died, add the wine, and bring to the boil, then simmer until reduced by half. Whisk in the crème fraîche and stir until smooth. Arrange the pheasant on a bed of cooked spinach, and surround with the apples and Herby Potatoes. Pour over the sauce.

COOK'S TIP
Chicken or guinea fowl breasts make a delicious alternative to pheasant.

CHOCOLATE & COFFEE CHEESECAKE

🥄 30 MINUTES 🍲 35 MINUTES 🧊 8 HOURS CHILLING

INGREDIENTS

100G (3½OZ) UNSALTED BUTTER, MELTED
250G (8OZ) AMARETTI BISCUITS, CRUSHED TO FINE CRUMBS
125G (4OZ) FLAKED ALMONDS, TOASTED & FINELY CHOPPED
750G (1½LB) FULL-FAT SOFT CHEESE, SOFTENED
175G (6OZ) CASTER SUGAR
3 LARGE EGGS, LIGHTLY BEATEN
3 LEMONS, GRATED ZEST
2 TSP VANILLA EXTRACT
3 TBSP INSTANT COFFEE GRANULES, DISSOLVED IN 1 TBSP HOT WATER
150G (5OZ) PLAIN DARK CHOCOLATE, MELTED
125ML (4OZ) WHIPPING CREAM, WARMED
SINGLE CREAM & COFFEE LIQUEUR TO SERVE

1 To make the base, mix the butter with the amaretti and almonds in a food processor. Turn the mixture into a 23cm (9in) lined and greased spring-form cake tin, pressing it around the base and sides with the back of a spoon.

2 Preheat oven to 180°C/350°F/Gas 4. For the filling, beat the soft cheese with the sugar until just smooth. Add the eggs, lemon zest, and vanilla and beat until just blended. Divide the mixture into 2 bowls. Into one of the bowls, stir in the coffee. Into the other, stir the melted chocolate and cream.

3 Cover the biscuit base with a large spoonful of the coffee mixture, followed by a large spoonful of the chocolate and cream mixture. Repeat until both are used up. With the end of a spoon, swirl the mixture around to create a marbled effect.

4 Place the cake in the middle of the oven and bake for 30 minutes. Allow to cool, then refrigerate for 8 hours or more in the tin. Release the sides of the tin, and serve with single cream flavoured with coffee liqueur.

COOK'S TIP
The cake will not appear cooked when it is first removed from the oven, but will set as it chills. It is very rich and could serve 10–12 in small slices.

WINTER DINNER FOR 6

PRAWN, LEEK & SAFFRON SOUP

 15 MINUTES   30 MINUTES

INGREDIENTS
24 RAW TIGER PRAWNS, ABOUT 400G (13OZ)
150G (5OZ) BUTTER
6 LEEKS, COARSELY CHOPPED
4 TBSP BRANDY
500ML (17FL OZ) WHITE VERMOUTH OR
DRY WHITE WINE
500ML (17FL OZ) FISH STOCK (SEE PAGE 185)
1 BAY LEAF
3 TBSP FRESH DILL, FINELY CHOPPED, PLUS
SPRIGS TO GARNISH
1 TSP SAFFRON THREADS, CRUSHED
SALT & PEPPER TO TASTE
200ML (7FL OZ) DOUBLE CREAM

1 Prepare the prawns (see Step 1, page 94). Heat the butter in a medium-sized saucepan, add the leeks, and cook gently for about 7 minutes, until softened. Add the brandy. After 10 seconds, carefully set light to it, then allow the flame to go out.

2 Add the vermouth, fish stock, bay leaf, chopped dill, and saffron, bring to the boil and simmer for 20 minutes. Remove the bay leaf; season. Blend the soup in a food processor until smooth, and return to the pan.

3 Add the prawns and cook for 2 minutes, until they turn pink. Stir in the cream and heat through until almost boiling. Serve in warmed soup bowls, garnished with sprigs of dill.

COOK'S TIP
One teaspoon of loosely packed saffron threads is equal to a quarter teaspoon of ground saffron.

FLEMISH-STYLE BEEF

 25 MINUTES   3 HOURS 15 MINUTES

INGREDIENTS
1.75KG (3½ LB) PIECE OF SIRLOIN BEEF
SALT TO TASTE
1 TBSP VEGETABLE OIL
4 ONIONS, COARSELY CHOPPED
4 GARLIC CLOVES, FINELY CHOPPED
4 CARROTS, CUT IN THICK SLICES
4 CLOVES, CRUSHED
½ ORANGE, ZEST ONLY (IN STRIPS)
4 TBSP BRANDY
1.25 LITRES (2PT) STOUT OR BEST BITTER
1 TBSP PEPPERCORNS, CRUSHED
2 BAY LEAVES
4 SPRIGS FRESH THYME
2 TBSP DRIED PORCINI, GROUND (OPTIONAL)
4 TBSP RED WINE VINEGAR
2 TBSP CORNFLOUR
2 TBSP SOFT BROWN SUGAR
BRAISED FENNEL & NEW POTATOES TO SERVE

1 Preheat oven to 160°C/325°F/Gas 3. Season the beef with salt. Heat the oil in a large frying pan and brown on all sides for approximately 5 minutes. Transfer to a casserole just large enough for the beef and vegetables. Return the frying pan to the heat.

2 Gently fry the onions, garlic, carrots, cloves, and orange zest for 5 minutes, spoon them into the casserole, surrounding the meat.

3 Place the casserole over a medium heat. Pour in the brandy and carefully set it alight. When the flames have died, add the stout, peppercorns, bay leaves, thyme, and ground porcini, if using. Bring to the boil.

4 Place a sheet of foil over the casserole, then cover it with the lid. Cook in the oven for 3 hours. When done, transfer the beef and vegetables to a carving plate and keep warm. Reserve the juices in the casserole.

5 To make the sauce, mix the vinegar, cornflour, and sugar in a bowl until smooth. Add 2 tablespoons of the meat juices and mix well. Pour into the casserole and cook over a low heat for 10 minutes, stirring constantly. Carve and serve the beef and vegetables with braised fennel and new potatoes.

COOK'S TIP
Cook this dish a day or two ahead for an even better flavour. Reheat in a moderate oven.

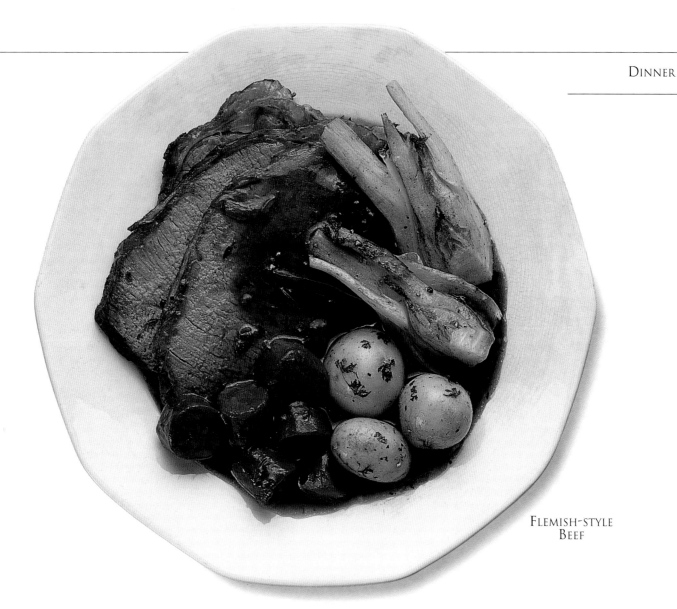

FLEMISH-STYLE
BEEF

STEAMED CRANBERRY PUDDING

🥄 30 MINUTES   🍲 1 HOUR 35 MINUTES

INGREDIENTS
175G (6OZ) BUTTER
200G (7OZ) CASTER SUGAR
175G (6OZ) SELF-RAISING FLOUR, SIFTED
1 TSP BAKING POWDER, SIFTED
3 LARGE EGGS, LIGHTLY BEATEN
2 LIMES, JUICE & GRATED ZEST
300G (10OZ) CRANBERRIES
4 TBSP MARMALADE
250ML (8FL OZ) ORANGE JUICE
2 TBSP ICING SUGAR, SIFTED
2 TSP ANGOSTURA BITTERS

1 Cream the butter and 175g (6oz) of the caster sugar until pale and fluffy. Add the flour, baking powder, eggs, half of the lime juice and zest, and 125g (4oz) of the cranberries, coarsely chopped. Mix well.

2 Grease a 2 litre (3pint) pudding basin, then sprinkle the remaining caster sugar over the interior. Cover the base with 60g (2oz) cranberries, spoon over the marmalade, then add the sponge mixture.

3 Cover the top of the basin with lightly buttered greaseproof paper, then cover this with a large sheet of foil that has been pleated once to allow the pudding to expand. Tie tightly in position with string. Steam over gently simmering water in a large closed pan for 1 hour 30 minutes.

4 To make the sauce, blend the remaining cranberries and lime juice and zest with the orange juice, icing sugar, and bitters. Heat and serve with the pudding.

COOK'S TIP
You can use a soufflé dish instead of a pudding basin to cook this sponge.

FAMILY GATHERING FOR 12

ITALIAN CABBAGE SOUP

15 MINUTES   17 MINUTES

INGREDIENTS
1 TBSP VEGETABLE OIL
300G (10OZ) SMOKED PANCETTA OR SMOKED
STREAKY BACON, DERINDED & SLICED
1 SAVOY CABBAGE, COARSELY CHOPPED
2 LITRES (3¼ PT) CHICKEN STOCK (SEE
PAGE 185)
SALT & PEPPER TO TASTE
500G (1LB) GRUYÈRE CHEESE, CUBED
250G (8OZ) WHITE BREAD, CRUSTS REMOVED,
CUT INTO 2CM (¾ IN) CUBES
10 SPRIGS EACH FRESH THYME & MARJORAM
2 BAY LEAVES
200G (7OZ) BUTTER, IN PIECES

1 Heat the oil in a frying pan, add the pancetta, and sauté over a moderate heat for 10 minutes, until crisp. Drain on kitchen paper.

2 Cook the cabbage in a large saucepan of salted boiling water for 2 minutes. Refresh under cold water and drain.

3 Heat the stock until it comes to the boil. Adjust seasoning to taste.

4 In a large saucepan, place in layers one third of the cabbage, followed by one third each of the Gruyère, bread, pancetta, and herbs. Repeat these layers twice more.

5 Pour over the boiling stock and bring back to the boil over a high heat. Add the butter pieces and simmer for 5 minutes. Discard the bay leaves and thyme stalks and serve immediately, without stirring the soup.

COOK'S TIPS
Serve the soup using a mug with a handle to dip deep into the pan. Halve the recipe to make a homely winter supper dish for 6 people.

SPICY PORK ROAST

25 MINUTES   2 HOURS   24 HOURS MARINATING

INGREDIENTS
175ML (6FL OZ) SUNFLOWER OIL
150ML (¼ PT) DARK RUM
150ML (¼ PT) LIGHT SOY SAUCE
150ML (¼ PT) CLEAR HONEY
2 LIMES, JUICE & GRATED ZEST
6 GARLIC CLOVES, CRUSHED
2 TBSP GROUND BLACK PEPPER
2 TBSP PAPRIKA
1 TBSP FENNEL SEEDS, CRUSHED
2 TSP GROUND GINGER
2KG (4LB) LOIN OF PORK
24 SHALLOTS, ABOUT 400G (13OZ), PEELED
750G (1½ LB) CARROTS, CUT INTO CHUNKS
10 SPRIGS FRESH THYME
4 BAY LEAVES
BAY ROAST POTATOES (SEE PAGE 187) TO SERVE

1 To make the marinade, place 150ml (¼ pint) of the oil, rum, soy sauce, honey, lime juice and zest, garlic, pepper, paprika, fennel, and ginger in a large non-metallic bowl. Mix well.

2 Pierce the pork all over with a sharp fork and rub the marinade into the meat. Cover and leave to marinate in the refrigerator for 24 hours, turning occasionally.

3 Preheat oven to 160°C/325°F/Gas 3. Remove the pork and reserve the marinade. Heat the remaining oil in a frying pan and, when it is fairly hot, brown the pork on all sides.

4 In a large casserole, place the pork and the marinade. Surround the pork with the shallots, carrots, and the herbs. Cover with a sheet of foil and the casserole lid.

5 Cook the pork in the oven for 2 hours. Baste and turn the meat approximately every 30 minutes. Carve the meat into slices 5mm (¼ in) thick and serve with the carrots and shallots, and Bay Roast Potatoes.

COOK'S TIP
If the liquid almost disappears in roasting, add two to three tablespoons of water.

MIRACULOUS BLACKBERRY CAKE

⏱ 1 HOUR 45 MINUTES · 🍲 1 HOUR 25 MINUTES

INGREDIENTS

7 EGGS: 3 WHITES ONLY, 4 WHOLE
PINCH OF CREAM OF TARTAR
175G (6OZ) LIGHT MUSCOVADO SUGAR, SIFTED
250G (8OZ) BUTTER, SOFTENED
250G (8OZ) CASTER SUGAR
250G (8OZ) SELF-RAISING FLOUR, SIFTED
2 TSP BAKING POWDER, SIFTED
2 TSP VANILLA EXTRACT
450ML (¾ PT) DOUBLE CREAM
2 TBSP CRÈME DE MÛRE (OPTIONAL)
3 TBSP BLACKBERRY JAM
175G (6OZ) BLACKBERRIES

1 To make the meringue, preheat oven to 140°C/275°F/Gas 1. Whisk the egg whites with cream of tartar until they form soft peaks. Gradually add the muscovado sugar, whisking after each addition, until the peaks hold firm.

2 With a pencil, draw 2 x 19cm (7½in) circles on greaseproof paper and place each on a baking sheet. Using a plain 1cm (½in) nozzle, pipe the meringue mixture, starting at the circle centres and spiralling outwards as far as the pencil lines. Bake for 1 hour. Set the meringues aside to cool.

3 Preheat oven to 180°C/350°F/Gas 4. For the sponge, beat the butter, caster sugar, flour, baking powder, eggs, and vanilla. Spoon the mixture into 2 lined and greased 20cm (8in) spring-form cake tins. Bake for 30 minutes. Leave the cakes in their tins for 10 minutes, then transfer to a wire rack.

4 Whisk together the cream and Crème de Mûre, if using, until stiff peaks have formed. Spread jam over the surface of each sponge.

5 Place a cake on a serving plate and spread one fifth of the cream over the jam. Lay one meringue on top and, again, spread with one fifth of the cream. Add the second cake and repeat the layers, finishing with the cream. Top with blackberries and cream piping made from the rest of the cream.

COOK'S TIPS

The meringue and sponges can be made a day in advance and stored in airtight containers. However, it is best to assemble the cake at the last moment, as the cream and berries will soften the meringue.

MIRACULOUS
BLACKBERRY CAKE

COUNTRY FOOD FOR 6

ASPARAGUS & HAM FETTUCINE

 10 MINUTES — 15 MINUTES

INGREDIENTS
375G (12OZ) ASPARAGUS SPEARS
2 TBSP OLIVE OIL
125G (4OZ) SMOKED HAM, SLICED
2 GARLIC CLOVES, SKINS LEFT ON, CRUSHED
UNDER THE FLAT OF A KNIFE
125G (4OZ) FROZEN PEAS, THAWED
625G (1¼LB) FETTUCINE
200ML (7FL OZ) WHIPPING CREAM
½ TSP GRATED NUTMEG
100G (3½OZ) PARMESAN CHEESE, GRATED,
PLUS EXTRA FOR TOPPING
SALT & PEPPER TO TASTE

1 Cut any woody ends off the asparagus spears. Cook in a saucepan of salted boiling water for 6 minutes, or until *al dente*. Drain.

2 Heat the olive oil in a frying pan. Add the ham and garlic and cook for 3 minutes, until the ham just begins to brown, then add the peas and asparagus. Cook for another 2 minutes.

3 Cook the fettucine in a large saucepan with plenty of salted

boiling water for 6 minutes if dried, 5–6 minutes if fresh, until *al dente*.

4 Drain the pasta, then return it to the pan. Add the cream and heat through, stirring constantly, until it begins to thicken. Stir in the asparagus and ham mixture, nutmeg, Parmesan, and seasoning. Serve immediately, with a little Parmesan sprinkled over the top of each portion.

VEGETABLE & NUT KEBABS

35 MINUTES — 1 HOUR 5 MINUTES

INGREDIENTS
250G (8OZ) SMALL POTATOES, SCRUBBED
250G (8OZ) OF EACH OF THE FOLLOWING, CUT
INTO CHUNKS: PUMPKIN (DESEEDED), SQUASH
(DESEEDED), CELERIAC, TURNIPS, PARSNIPS
150ML (¼PT) OLIVE OIL
5 TBSP PLAIN FLOUR
SALT & PEPPER TO TASTE
250G (8OZ) BRAZIL NUTS
3 TBSP WATER
3 SHALLOTS, COARSELY CHOPPED
3 GARLIC CLOVES, COARSELY CHOPPED
2.5CM (1IN) PIECE OF FRESH GINGER, PEELED
& COARSELY CHOPPED
90G (3OZ) ROASTED PEANUTS (UNSALTED)
1 TBSP FENNEL SEEDS
500ML (17FL OZ) COCONUT MILK
GREEN SALAD LEAVES & WALNUT DRESSING
(SEE PAGE 185) TO SERVE

1 Bring a large saucepan of salted water to the boil, add all the vegetables, bring back to the boil, then drain immediately.

2 Preheat oven to 220°C/425°F/Gas 7. As soon as the vegetables are cool enough to handle, toss them in 2 tablespoons of oil, then roll in flour. Thread alternately onto long skewers, allowing 3 per person.

3 Coat the bases of 2 baking sheets in olive oil, about 3 tablespoons per sheet, and heat in the oven. When the oil is hot, lay the kebabs onto the sheets. Bake for 45 minutes, turning the kebabs once. Add the Brazil nuts 20 minutes before the end of cooking.

4 Meanwhile, make the sauce. In a food processor, blend the water with the shallots, garlic, ginger, peanuts, fennel seeds, and salt.

5 Heat the remaining oil in a frying pan and add the processed sauce ingredients. Fry gently for 5 minutes, then stir in the coconut milk. Cook uncovered over a low heat for 10 minutes. Serve the kebabs and Brazil nuts with the sauce and a green leaf salad with Walnut Dressing.

COOK'S TIP
If the vegetables appear to be browning too much during cooking, cover loosely with foil.

SPICED QUINCES
& EARL GREY
SORBET

SPICED QUINCES & EARL GREY SORBET

10 MINUTES · 40 MINUTES · 12 HOURS CHILLING

INGREDIENTS

2 LARGE QUINCES
750ML (1¼ PT) SWEET WHITE WINE
2 LEMONS, JUICE & GRATED ZEST
2 SPRIGS FRESH ROSEMARY
4 TBSP CLEAR HONEY (PREFERABLY ACACIA)
3 EARL GREY TEA BAGS
375G (12OZ) WATER
375G (12OZ) SUGAR
2 LIMES, JUICE & GRATED ZEST, RESERVING
ZEST TO DECORATE
1 LARGE EGG, WHITE ONLY

COOK'S TIPS

If quinces are unavailable, use pears (preferably Comice variety) instead. If using an ice cream maker, follow the manufacturer's instructions.

1 To make the spiced quinces, cut the fruit into quarters, remove the cores, then cut each quarter into 3 wedge-shaped slices.

2 In a saucepan, heat half of the wine (chill the rest for the sorbet). Add the quinces, lemon juice and zest, rosemary, honey, and 1 tea bag.

3 Poach the quinces for 15–20 minutes, until they are just cooked. Discard the tea bag and transfer the quince slices to a serving dish.

4 Return the pan to the heat and reduce the liquid to about 6 tablespoons. Pour it over the quinces and refrigerate overnight.

5 To make the sorbet, heat the water in a saucepan with the sugar and 2 tea bags. Bring almost to the boil, stirring until the sugar has dissolved to make a syrup. Discard the tea bags. Allow syrup to cool, then refrigerate for at least 2 hours, until well chilled.

6 Pour the syrup, juice and zest of 2 limes, and the remaining wine into a rigid freezerproof container, cover, and freeze for 3 hours, stirring at the end of each hour. On the final stirring, lightly beat the egg white and stir into the sorbet. Refreeze for at least 3 hours. Transfer to the refrigerator 30 minutes before serving to soften. Decorate with lime zest and serve with the quinces.

BUFFET
PARTIES

WINING AND DINING MORE THAN TWELVE GUESTS IS MOST SIMPLY EXECUTED WITH A BUFFET. THERE ARE PLENTY OF EASY DISHES YOU CAN PREPARE WELL IN ADVANCE OR, IF YOU PREFER TO LIVE DANGEROUSLY, AFTER YOUR GUESTS HAVE ARRIVED! PLAN AND ADHERE TO A METICULOUS WORK SCHEDULE, COOK FLAVOURSOME FOOD THAT IS SIMPLE TO EAT, AND A RELAXED AND SOCIABLE CELEBRATION WILL BE ASSURED.

The Champagne Buffet menu (page 113), with its Marinated Salmon, Chicken Crêpe Gâteau, and Savarin, is especially appropriate for Christmas celebrations (right).

CHRISTMAS

Pile the tables with delectable treats – it is

FOLLOW OR ADAPT the many decorative
traditions the festive season
has to offer to make your
Christmas party memorable.

WRAPPING PAPER

Make simple gift wrap using tissue paper and
spray paints. Follow the steps below, or create
a random effect by crumpling up the paper
before you spray.

PERSONAL GIFTS
*A gift that is stylishly
wrapped in customized
paper becomes even more of
a treat for the recipient.*

1 For paper with a bold square pattern,
pleat a sheet of coloured tissue paper
to make 2–5cm (¾–2in) folds. The pattern
varies according to the width of the folds.

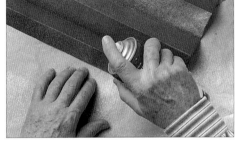

2 Place the paper in a cardboard box or
on newspaper in a well-ventilated area.
Release the folds (but do not smooth flat)
and spray paint across the front of each one.

3 Allow the paint to dry, then pleat the
paper again at right angles to the first
folds. Repeat Step 2, using a different
coloured paint if you wish.

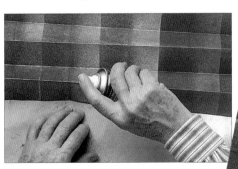

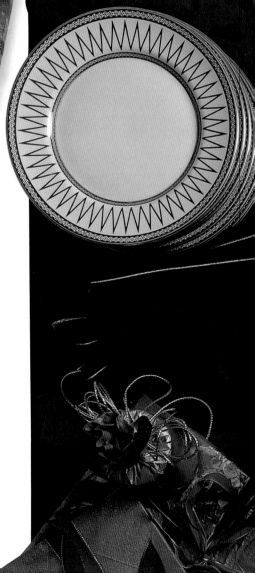

time to celebrate

MAROON BREAD BASKET
Line a basket with a colour-co-ordinated napkin to make a country loaf cut into wedges as much a decoration as a part of the meal.

LAYOUT OF THE TABLE
The buffet table, placed against a wall, is arranged with the items needed for each course grouped together. Any decorative elements are out of the way, at the back.

FRUIT ARRANGEMENT
A terracotta bowl brimming with fruit, a few candles, and a few simple flowers is an impressive decoration for a festive buffet table.

A CHRISTMAS TREE FOR THE WALL

Hang this long-lasting Christmas tree, decorated with fruit and glittering lights, on the wall like a picture, where it will not take up much space. The frame and its chicken wire covering are easy to assemble and can be kept to re-use from year to year, replacing the moss and foliage. Suspend nuts, chocolates, and shop-bought decorations on the tree, too.

1 ◁ Make a triangular frame from three pieces of bamboo, two the same length and one slightly shorter, wired together with florists' stub wires. Cover the frame with a double layer of chicken wire.

2 ▷ Twist the open ends of the chicken wire together to secure it around the frame, leaving a gap through which to fill with sphagnum moss. Pack the frame with moss, then close the gap.

Moss must be firm, but not too compacted

3 ▷ Poke sprigs of conifer – here silver fir as it does not drop its needles – into the moss-filled frame. Start at the bottom with larger pieces, overlapping to cover as you work up.

4 ▷ Thread a wire through each fruit, hooking one end and pulling it back gently into the fruit. Poke the free wire end through the frame from the front; bend at the back to secure.

5 ▷ Make holes for the fairy lights with a pencil. Starting at the top with the non-plug end, push each bulb through from the back, keeping the flex at the back and finishing with the plug near the tree's base.

Attach a hanging hook at top

Wire on a piece of bark for the trunk

108

Lime

DECORATIONS
*The tree is hung with limes,
vine tomatoes, and white
aubergines, which can be
replaced if they look tired.*

CHRISTMAS CONIFERS
*Although conifers such as the
silver fir here are usually
associated with Christmas,
other evergreens – laurel and
skimmia, perhaps – would
make an attractive change.*

Vine Tomato

*White
Aubergine*

ALFRESCO

"The greatest dishes are very simple dishes"

WHEN THE WEATHER IS FAIR, serve an appetizing and relaxed buffet lunch outdoors in your garden. Set it up out of the sun but near the house, so that hot food does not cool too much on its way to the table.

ICE BOWL

Very beautiful, yet simple to make, ice bowls last for over an hour in the shade, once out of the freezer. Choose plants that are in season.

Alstroemeria — Sweet Pea

Eustoma

St John's Wort

1 Place one bowl inside another 3–4cm (1¼–1¾ in) larger in diameter. Half fill the outer bowl with water, adding a little milk or food colouring for a frosted effect.

2 Gently fill the inner bowl with water so that it sinks to the same level as the outer bowl. Hold it straight in a central position, and secure with adhesive tape.

3 Wedge non-toxic plant material into the water. Freeze for at least 8 hours. To release, pour cold water into the inner bowl, partially submerge the outer bowl in cold, never warm, water. After a minute, ease the ice bowl free.

  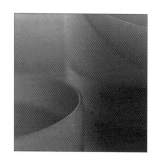

GEORGE AUGUSTE ESCOFFIER 1846–1935

CHILLI POT
Fill little terracotta pots with chillis emerging from a ruff of hebe foliage, their ends fanned out like a fountain. Being small, pots do not clutter the table.

FROSTED SERVING BOWL
An ice bowl is a fitting and attractive receptacle from which to serve sorbets and ice creams. Fill with scoops of softened ice cream just before serving.

MENUS
The tables groan with food and the guests

BIRTHDAY PARTY
❧

Hearty cassoulet is a meal all by itself, but team it with the lightest of chocolate birthday cakes for a special celebration. *Serves 18*

CASSOULET
Haricot beans and tender meats are all perfumed with herbs to make up this unusual dish from southwest France.

CHOCOLATE BIRTHDAY CAKE
This beautifully decorated flourless cake is somehow both rich and very light.

DRINKS
Partner the cassoulet with a good dry Graves, which comes from the same part of France. A demi-sec Champagne served with the birthday cake is both delicious and good for toasting.

PLANNING NOTES
The cassoulet improves with time; keep it covered in the refrigerator for a couple of days. Thoroughly heat it through in a moderate oven when required. If the cassoulet seems dry, add enough white wine to make the mixture just moist, while it is cooking. The cake and its chocolate covering are best eaten within two days. *See pages 114–15 for recipes.*

ALL ITALIAN
❧

A vegetarian and a seafood pasta, followed by ice bowls of ice cream, make a colourful feast for a small buffet party. *Serves 12*

BROCCOLI & PINE NUT FETTUCINE
A colourful pasta with the sharp flavour of lemon.

PRAWN & MUSHROOM PAPARDELLE
This dish is delicious in its mix of tastes and textures.

COFFEE & AMARETTO ICE CREAM
The creamy blend of coffee and almond is not too sweet.

DRINKS
A dry sparkling Prosecco from the Veneto would provide just the right splash of vino to complement the pasta. For an extra special treat, serve sweet Vin Santo with the ice cream – the apricot flavoured variety would be excellent.

PLANNING NOTES
Make the ice cream up to six weeks in advance. Both pasta sauces can be prepared up to eight hours ahead; quickly heat each one through in the pasta saucepan while the pasta drains in a colander. Pasta tastes best immediately after cooking, but at least it is easy to cook. Toss the pasta back in with the sauce and serve in warmed pasta bowls. The prawns must be cooked at the last minute. *See pages 116–17 for recipes.*

are happy

CHAMPAGNE BUFFET

A festive trio of elegant dishes that can be prepared in advance for a special occasion. *Serves 18*

MARINATED SALMON
Home-prepared gravadlax with a luscious herbed-mustard sauce.

CHICKEN CRÊPE GÂTEAU
An impressive tower of crêpes layered with chicken, ham, and asparagus in a creamy wine sauce.

FRESH FRUIT SAVARIN
A rum-soaked ring of sweet yeasted bread filled with fruits soaked in rum and lime.

DRINKS
This is a feast that calls out for Champagne. Before the meal, start with Champagne cocktails (see page 135 for recipes), followed by a vintage Champagne with the salmon and the chicken gâteau. A fine Sauternes makes a superb accompaniment for the savarin.

PLANNING NOTES
Prepare the sauce for the chicken gâteau up to eight hours in advance, but make the crêpes and assemble the gâteau just before baking. After baking, the gâteau can be frozen whole for up to six weeks. Defrost fully before heating for 30 minutes in a moderate oven. Make the savarin up to two days (but no more) in advance, as it improves with a day's soaking in its rum syrup. It can be frozen (without syrup) for up to six weeks. Prepare the salmon and its sauce up to three hours in advance and refrigerate. *See pages 118–19 for recipes.*

LUNCHEON

This light buffet would be perfect served on a summer day in glorious dappled shade.
Serves 12

HOME-BAKED OAT BISCUITS & CHEESE
Crumbly biscuits served with a selection of cheeses.

PORK WITH TUNA SAUCE
Eaten cold, this unlikely-sounding combination is exceptionally good.

WEST INDIAN PUNCH JELLY
An attractive mould with the flavours of exotic fruits and rum.

DRINKS
With the cheeses and the pork, choose a Semillon Chardonnay, and to accompany the jelly, a sweet Muscat. The orange-flavoured Muscat is my particular favourite.

PLANNING NOTES
Bake the biscuits a day in advance, and store in an airtight tin. The pork needs to marinate for at least 24 hours, but do not make it more than 36 hours ahead. Prepare the jelly the day before, and keep it in the refrigerator until you are ready to serve. *See pages 120–21 for recipes.*

BIRTHDAY PARTY FOR 18

CASSOULET

🥄 35 MINUTES   🍲 2 HOURS 55 MINUTES   ⬜ 12 HOURS SOAKING

INGREDIENTS

1.25KG (2½LB) BONED SHOULDER OF LAMB
500ML (17FL OZ) DRY WHITE WINE
6 ONIONS, COARSELY CHOPPED
8 SPRIGS MARJORAM, PLUS 3 TBSP FRESH
MARJORAM, FINELY CHOPPED (OR 2 TSP DRIED)
1KG (2LB) DRIED HARICOT BEANS, SOAKED FOR
12 HOURS, RINSED & DRAINED
375G (12OZ) SMOKED PANCETTA OR SMOKED
STREAKY BACON, DERINDED & SLICED
1.25KG (2½LB) CANNED PLUM TOMATOES
3 LARGE CARROTS, CUT INTO CHUNKS
1 LEMON, ZEST ONLY, CUT INTO THIN STRIPS
4 GARLIC CLOVES, SKINS LEFT ON, CRUSHED
UNDER THE FLAT OF A KNIFE
3 BAY LEAVES
750G (1½LB) TOULOUSE SAUSAGES OR
COARSE 100% PORK SAUSAGES
750G (1½LB) DUCK BREASTS, SKINNED
2 TBSP OLIVE OIL (IF FRYING)
SALT & PEPPER TO TASTE
250G (8OZ) FRESH WHITE BREADCRUMBS
4 TBSP FLAT-LEAF PARSLEY, COARSELY CHOPPED
GREEN SALAD LEAVES TO SERVE

1 Preheat oven to 190°C/375°F/Gas 5. Place the lamb in a large roasting tin with the wine, half the onions, and the marjoram sprigs. Bake in the oven for 1 hour 50 minutes.

2 Meanwhile, make the bean mixture. Place the pre-soaked beans in a large saucepan, cover with lightly salted water, bring to the boil and boil steadily for 15 minutes. Drain.

3 Return the beans to the pan and add the pancetta, tomatoes, carrots, lemon zest, remaining onions, 3 garlic cloves, and the chopped marjoram and bay leaves. Cover with water, bring to the boil, then simmer, covered, for 1 hour, stirring occasionally.

4 Brown the sausages and duck breasts under the grill or cook in a large frying pan with oil. Add them to the bean and vegetable mixture, cover, and cook over a moderate heat for a further 30 minutes.

5 Remove the saucepan from the heat, then drain, reserving the liquid, but discarding the garlic cloves. Adjust seasoning. Once cool enough to handle, cut the sausages and duck into bite-sized chunks.

6 When the lamb is cooked, remove from the oven and set aside to cool. Turn the oven to 180°C/350°F/Gas 4. Trim the lamb of excess fat and cut it

into bite-sized chunks. Reserve the liquid but discard the onions and marjoram sprigs.

7 Rub the insides of 2 large casseroles with the remaining garlic clove, then arrange the bean and vegetable mixture, sausage, duck, and lamb in alternating layers, finishing with a layer of beans and vegetables. Pour over the wine and juices from the lamb and the reserved liquid from the beans and vegetables.

8 In a small bowl, combine the breadcrumbs and parsley. Take half the mixture and sprinkle it over the surface of both casseroles.

9 Bake for 20 minutes, then push the crumbs down into the liquid and sprinkle the remaining breadcrumb mixture over each dish. Bake for a further 45 minutes (1 hour 5 minutes in total), allowing the layer of breadcrumbs to brown. Serve with a green leaf salad.

COOK'S TIPS

In the final dish, the meat and beans should be just moist; you may need to add a little more wine in the last 30 minutes of cooking. You can substitute 750g (1½lb) canned confit of duck for the duck breasts; as confit is already cooked, add it in Step 7. The dish can be prepared to Step 8 two days in advance, and finished on the day.

CHOCOLATE BIRTHDAY CAKE

⏲ 30 MINUTES 🍲 1 HOUR 50 MINUTES

INGREDIENTS

875G (1¾ LB) PLAIN DARK CHOCOLATE
12 LARGE EGGS: 9 SEPARATED, 3 WHOLE
375G (12OZ) CASTER SUGAR
300G (10OZ) GROUND HAZELNUTS
2 TBSP INSTANT COFFEE GRANULES, DISSOLVED
IN 1 TBSP HOT WATER, COOLED
3 TBSP COFFEE LIQUEUR (OPTIONAL)
PINCH OF CREAM OF TARTAR
175G (6OZ) UNSALTED BUTTER

COOK'S TIPS

If you are using a microwave, 500g (1lb) of chocolate broken in pieces will take about 6 minutes to melt on medium. The cake can be made a day in advance, and coated on the day, but it is best eaten within 24 hours of making. Crystallized Petals or Chocolate Leaves (page 170) can be used instead of fresh petals for decoration.

CHOCOLATE
BIRTHDAY CAKE

1 Preheat oven to 180°C/350°/Gas 4. Break 500g (1lb) of the chocolate into small pieces, then heat in a double boiler, heatproof bowl over a saucepan of simmering water, or microwave. Stir gently (do not beat) as it melts until smooth. Leave to cool.

2 Whisk the egg yolks, whole eggs, and sugar until pale and fluffy.

3 Gently fold the melted chocolate and ground hazelnuts into the egg mixture, then the cooled coffee and coffee liqueur, if using. In another bowl, whisk the egg whites and cream of tartar until they form stiff peaks,

then add them to the cake mixture. Spoon the mixture into a lined and greased 25cm (10in) round cake tin.

4 Bake on the lowest shelf of the oven for 1 hour 20 minutes. Leave the cake in its tin for 10 minutes, then turn it out onto a wire rack to cool.

5 To make the covering, heat the butter and remaining chocolate as in Step 1, stirring very gently until smooth. Leave to cool for about 5 minutes, so that it thickens slightly.

6 With the cake still upside down, spread the chocolate mixture over the surface of the cake and around the sides. Leave the covering to set, then transfer to a cake plate and decorate with fresh flower petals.

ALL ITALIAN FOR 12

BROCCOLI & PINE NUT FETTUCINE

 10 MINUTES 15 MINUTES

INGREDIENTS
1.25KG (2½LB) BROCCOLI
175G (6OZ) BUTTER
24 LEAVES FRESH SAGE, SHREDDED
3 LEMONS, FINELY SLICED FRUIT OF ½,
JUICE & GRATED ZEST OF 2½
60G (2OZ) PICKLED LEMON SLICES (OPTIONAL)
SALT & PEPPER TO TASTE
1KG (2LB) FETTUCINE
90G (3OZ) PINE NUTS, LIGHTLY TOASTED
PARMESAN CHEESE, GRATED FOR TOPPING

1 Trim the broccoli, and cut the larger florets in half. Cook in a saucepan of salted boiling water for 3 minutes. Refresh under cold water and drain.

2 Heat the butter in a large frying pan until it just begins to brown. Immediately add the broccoli, sage, lemon slices, and pickled lemon (if using). Fry gently over a low heat for 5 minutes, until warmed through, then add the lemon juice and zest. Adjust the seasoning.

3 Cook the fettucine in 2 large saucepans with plenty of salted boiling water for 6 minutes if dried, 5–6 minutes if fresh, until *al dente*. Drain, then return it to the 2 pans. Add half each of the broccoli mixture and pine nuts to each pan, and toss. Serve immediately, sprinkled with Parmesan.

COOK'S TIP
Use two very large saucepans of lightly salted boiling water for the pasta as it needs to be uncrowded when it cooks.

PRAWN & MUSHROOM PAPARDELLE

 30 MINUTES 25 MINUTES

INGREDIENTS
500G (1LB) RAW TIGER PRAWNS
500ML (17FL OZ) WATER
5 TBSP OLIVE OIL
4 GARLIC CLOVES, FINELY CHOPPED
6 PLUM TOMATOES, SKINNED
& FINELY CHOPPED
3 TBSP TOMATO PURÉE
250G (8OZ) FIELD OR SHITAKE
MUSHROOMS, SLICED
2 TSP GROUND BLACK PEPPER
SALT TO TASTE
1KG (2LB) PAPARDELLE OR FETTUCINE
250G (8OZ) MASCARPONE CHEESE
FRESH BASIL, SHREDDED, TO GARNISH
TOMATO & BASIL SALAD TO SERVE

1 Prepare the prawns (see Step 1, page 94), reserving shells for stock.

2 To make the stock, crush the shells and place in a large saucepan with the water. Bring to the boil. Simmer for 30 minutes, until reduced by half. Strain and discard the shells.

3 To make the sauce, heat 3 tablespoons of the oil in a large saucepan over a moderate heat, then add the garlic. Cook for about 5 minutes, then add the tomatoes and tomato purée. Turn heat to low and cook for about 10 minutes.

4 Add the mushrooms, pepper, and stock. Bring to the boil and simmer for 5 minutes. Add the salt. Keep warm over a very low heat.

5 Cook the papardelle in 2 large saucepans with plenty of salted boiling water for 8–10 minutes if dried, 5–6 minutes if fresh, until *al dente*.

6 While the pasta is cooking, heat the remaining oil in a frying pan until very hot, then add the prawns and cook for about 1 minute each side, until they turn pink.

7 Drain the pasta, then return it to the 2 pans. Add half each of the prawns, sauce, and mascarpone to each pan, and toss. Garnish with basil and serve with a tomato and basil salad.

PRAWN &
MUSHROOM
PAPARDELLE

COFFEE & AMARETTO ICE CREAM

— 20 MINUTES — 10 MINUTES — 8 HOURS CHILLING —

INGREDIENTS

900ML (1½ PT) SINGLE CREAM, CHILLED
250G (8OZ) CASTER SUGAR
35G (1¼ OZ) INSTANT COFFEE GRANULES
750ML (1¼ PT) CRÈME FRAÎCHE
1 TBSP VANILLA EXTRACT
2 TSP GROUND NUTMEG
250G (8OZ) AMARETTI BISCUITS, CRUSHED
(⅔ COARSELY, ⅓ FINELY)
200ML (7FL OZ) MILK
60G (2OZ) UNSALTED BUTTER
200G (7OZ) PLAIN DARK CHOCOLATE,
BROKEN IN SMALL PIECES

1 To make the ice cream, heat 150ml (½ pint) of the cream with the sugar in a saucepan, stirring until the sugar dissolves. Add 20g (¾ oz) of the coffee. Leave to cool, then refrigerate for at least 2 hours, until thoroughly chilled.

2 Whisk in the remaining cream, crème fraîche, vanilla, and nutmeg.

3 Turn the mixture into a rigid freezerproof container, cover, and freeze for 3 hours, stirring at the end of each hour (follow the manufacturer's instructions if you use an ice cream maker). On the final stirring, add the coarse amaretti. Refreeze for 3 hours.

4 To make the sauce, heat the milk and butter in a saucepan and bring to the boil. Remove from the heat, then stir in the remaining coffee and the chocolate. Stir gently until mixed and allow to cool, stirring occasionally.

5 Transfer the ice cream to the refrigerator 30 minutes before eating to soften. To serve, sprinkle fine amaretti crumbs over the top and pour over the sauce.

117

CHAMPAGNE BUFFET FOR 18

MARINATED SALMON

⏱ 20 MINUTES   ☐ 2 HOURS 30 MINUTES CHILLING

INGREDIENTS

1KG (2LB) FRESH SALMON, BONED,
SKINNED, & FILLETED
6 LEMONS, JUICE & GRATED ZEST
OF 4, JUICE OF 2
350ML (12FL OZ) GRAPESEED OIL OR ANY
OTHER LIGHT OIL
30G (1OZ) FRESH DILL, FINELY CHOPPED,
PLUS SPRIGS TO GARNISH
1½ TSP SALT
½ TSP GROUND BLACK PEPPER
5 TBSP DIJON MUSTARD
1 TBSP CASTER SUGAR
CAPERS (OPTIONAL), TO GARNISH

1 Chill the salmon in the freezer for about 1 hour 30 minutes, until it is almost frozen. Cut very thin slices diagonally across the grain. Place on a large platter.

2 To make the marinade, combine the juice and grated zest of 4 lemons and 150ml (¼ pint) of the oil. Add half the chopped dill and 1 teaspoon of salt. Pour over the salmon slices. Sprinkle with pepper and leave, in the refrigerator, covered with clingfilm, for 1–18 hours.

3 To make the dressing, combine the mustard, juice of 2 lemons, sugar, remaining salt, and remaining chopped dill. Drizzle in 200ml (7fl oz) oil, a little at a time, beating constantly, or liquidize in a blender until smooth. Garnish each portion with a sprig of dill and capers, if using, and serve with the sauce and brown bread.

COOK'S TIP

If the salmon is well chilled it will slice much more easily. Alternatively, ask your fishmonger to slice it for you. Keep it well refrigerated until use.

CHICKEN CRÊPE GÂTEAU

⏱ 1 HOUR 5 MINUTES   🍲 1 HOUR

INGREDIENTS

475G (15OZ) PLAIN FLOUR, SIFTED
6 EGGS
2.8 LITRES (4½PT) MILK
90ML (3FL OZ) VEGETABLE OIL
2 TBSP FRESH THYME, FINELY CHOPPED
SALT & PEPPER TO TASTE
900ML (1½PT) DRY WHITE WINE
250G (8OZ) BUTTER
475G (15OZ) PARMESAN CHEESE, GRATED
2.25G (4½LB) COOKED CHICKEN, DICED
750G (1½LB) COOKED SMOKED HAM, DICED
36 ASPARAGUS SPEARS, COOKED AL DENTE

COOK'S TIPS

Each gâteau will serve about 6 people so you will need to make 3 for 18 guests. Once assembled, they can be frozen for 2 months. Defrost, then reheat for 30 minutes in a moderate oven.

1 To make the crêpe batter, blend in a food processor 300g (10oz) flour, eggs, 900ml (1½ pint) milk, oil, thyme, and seasoning. Beat until well mixed. Refrigerate for 30 minutes.

2 Meanwhile make the filling: bring the wine to the boil and reduce by about three-quarters. Add 175g (6oz) of the butter and the remaining flour, and mix to a smooth paste. Gradually add the remaining milk, stirring with each addition, until smooth. Cook gently for 15 minutes.

3 Stir in the Parmesan, reserving 90g (3oz), adjust the seasoning, then remove the sauce from the heat. Stir in the chicken and ham. Mix well.

4 Preheat oven to 200°C/400°F/Gas 6. Heat 1 teaspoon of butter in a 23cm (9in) frying pan until it just browns. Add 3 tablespoons of batter and cook the crêpe on both sides until golden. Repeat until the batter is used, re-greasing the pan between crêpes.

5 In a 23cm (9in) greased, loose-bottomed cake tin, make the first gâteau: lay 1 crêpe on the base, then cover it with about 8 tablespoons of filling. Repeat for 6 more layers, adding 6 asparagus spears on 2 of the layers. Finish with a crêpe and one-third of the remaining Parmesan. Assemble 2 more gâteaux. Bake for 30 minutes, allow to cool slightly, turn out, and serve warm.

FRESH FRUIT SAVARIN

20 MINUTES　1 HOUR　1 HOUR 45 MINUTES STANDING

INGREDIENTS

575G (1LB 2½OZ) CASTER SUGAR
300ML (½PT) MILK, WARMED
1 TBSP EASY-BLEND YEAST
500G (1LB) STRONG WHITE BREAD FLOUR,
SIFTED
6 LARGE EGGS, LIGHTLY BEATEN
2 TSP SALT
200G (7OZ) BUTTER, MELTED
600ML (1PT) WATER
200ML (7FL OZ) DARK RUM, KIRSCH,
OR BRANDY
EXOTIC OR SEASONAL FRESH FRUIT
CRÈME FRAÎCHE OR DOUBLE CREAM TO SERVE

COOK'S TIPS

If you are not using easy blend yeast, follow the instructions on the yeast packet. If the savarin is browning too quickly in the oven, cover it with greaseproof paper for the last 10 minutes of cooking. In summer, the savarin is very good served with mixed berries.

1 To make the savarin, place 75g (2½oz) of the sugar, the warmed milk, yeast, flour, eggs, and salt in a large, greased bowl, and beat well. Cover with clingfilm and a tea towel, and leave in a warm place for 1 hour, until doubled in size.

2 On a floured work surface, push down the dough and knead in the melted butter. Knead for about 10 minutes, until elastic, then place the dough in a greased and floured 30cm (12in) savarin mould. Cover with oiled clingfilm and leave to rise in a warm place for a further 45 minutes, until it is about level with the top of the tin. Preheat oven to 190°C/375°F/Gas 5.

3 Bake for 45 minutes. Leave to cool for 30 minutes, then ease it loose from its tin, but do not remove it yet.

4 While the savarin is baking, make the syrup. Place the water and remaining sugar in a saucepan and bring slowly to the boil, stirring until the sugar has dissolved. Boil for 15 minutes: do not allow the syrup to caramelize. Take off the heat and allow to cool slightly, then add the rum.

5 Prick the savarin all over with a skewer and drizzle over the syrup, reserving about 300ml (½ pint), until it is absorbed. When the savarin has cooled completely, turn it onto a 45cm (18in) serving platter. Fill the centre with fresh fruit. Slice and serve with the fruit, a spoonful of syrup, and crème fraîche or double cream.

FRESH FRUIT
SAVARIN

LUNCHEON FOR 12

HOME-BAKED OAT BISCUITS & CHEESE

15 MINUTES | 25 MINUTES

INGREDIENTS

125G (4OZ) PLAIN WHOLEMEAL FLOUR, SIFTED
150G (5OZ) MEDIUM OATMEAL, PLUS
EXTRA FOR DUSTING
150G (5OZ) PORRIDGE OATS
1½ TSP BAKING POWDER, SIFTED
1 TSP SALT
1 TBSP CASTER SUGAR
125G (4OZ) UNSALTED BUTTER, MELTED
3 TBSP COLD WATER

1 In a large mixing bowl, combine the flour, 150g (5oz) oatmeal, the porridge oats, baking powder, salt, and sugar. Make a well in the centre and pour in the melted butter. Mix well.

2 Add the cold water, a little at a time. Knead until well blended and the dough is firm and holds together. Divide the mixture in 2, and sprinkle oatmeal all over both pieces.

3 Preheat oven to 160°C/325°F/Gas 3. Line and grease 2 baking sheets. Dust a work surface with oatmeal and roll out the first piece of dough to about 3mm (⅛in) thick.

4 Dust the upper surface with oatmeal and roll it in gently. With a 5cm (2in) cutter, cut the dough into rounds. Place them 5mm (¼in) apart on the baking sheet.

5 Repeat for the remaining dough on the second sheet. Bake for 25 minutes, until the biscuits are golden, then transfer to a wire rack to cool.

COOK'S TIPS

These biscuits may be made 2 days in advance and stored in an airtight tin. Choose a mixture of soft and hard cow's milk and goat's milk cheeses to serve with the biscuits. Make sure that they are brought slowly to room temperature if they have been chilled.

HOME-BAKED OAT BISCUITS
WITH A SELECTION OF CHEESES
*Clockwise from right: Goat's Cheese,
Torta di Dolcelatte, Blue Shropshire,
Goat's Cheese, and Brie.*

PORK WITH TUNA SAUCE

20 MINUTES · 1 HOUR 45 MINUTES · 24 HOURS CHILLING

INGREDIENTS
45G (1½ OZ) BUTTER
325ML (11FL OZ) OLIVE OIL
1.5KG (3LB) BONED LOIN OF PORK
SALT & PEPPER TO TASTE
750ML (1¼ PT) MILK
3 BAY LEAVES
150ML (¼ PT) CRÈME FRAÎCHE
1 LEMON, JUICE ONLY
300G (10OZ) CANNED TUNA IN OIL, DRAINED
6 ANCHOVY FILLETS
6 TBSP CAPERS
150ML (¼ PT) MAYONNAISE (SEE PAGE 147)
TOMATO & BASIL SALAD TO SERVE

1 Heat the butter and 3 tablespoons of oil in a heavy casserole until the butter has melted. Put in the pork, skin side down. Add the seasoning. Brown well on both sides.

2 Add half of the milk and the bay leaves and bring to the boil, then simmer. Half cover the pan and cook for 1 hour, turning the pork once. Add the remaining milk. Cover and simmer very gently for a further 40 minutes. Remove the pork and leave it to cool, discarding the contents of the pan.

3 Meanwhile, make the sauce. Put the remaining oil, crème fraîche, lemon juice, tuna, anchovies, and

capers in a blender and liquidize until smooth. Fold the mixture into the Mayonnaise. Adjust seasoning.

4 Cut the pork into very thin slices. Spread a thin layer of sauce on the bottom of a large serving dish and place a layer of pork slices on top. Repeat until both the pork and sauce are used, finishing with a thin layer of sauce. Cover and refrigerate for 24 hours. Serve cold with a tomato and basil salad.

COOK'S TIP
In Italy, veal is traditionally used to make this dish and it can be substituted for the pork.

WEST INDIAN PUNCH JELLY

30 MINUTES · 5 MINUTES · 5 HOURS CHILLING

INGREDIENTS
3 TBSP POWDERED GELATINE
125ML (4FL OZ) WATER
500ML (17FL OZ) ORANGE JUICE
500ML (17FL OZ) PINEAPPLE JUICE
500ML (17FL OZ) MANGO JUICE
125G (4OZ) CASTER SUGAR
6 LIMES, JUICE ONLY
250ML (8FL OZ) WHITE RUM OR GRAPE JUICE
PLUS 1 TBSP RUM ESSENCE
½ TSP GRATED NUTMEG
36 LYCHEES (FRESH OR CANNED), SKINNED,
STONES REMOVED
TROPICAL FRUITS, SLICED, TO SERVE

1 Sprinkle the gelatine onto the water in a small saucepan. Leave to soak for 5 minutes. Place over a very low heat and stir until the gelatine has dissolved and the liquid is clear.

2 In a large saucepan, heat the orange, pineapple, and mango juices with the sugar, stirring gently until the sugar has dissolved.

3 Bring the liquid almost to the boil and add the gelatine. Stir well to mix. Reserve 2 tablespoons of the lime juice; add the remainder with the rum and nutmeg to the pan. Stir again.

4 Rinse 12 individual 200ml (7fl oz) moulds (or 2 x 1 litre moulds) in cold water, then half fill each, using

only half of the mixture. Leave to cool, then refrigerate for 1 hour 30 minutes. Leave the remaining mixture at room temperature.

5 Place 3 lychees in the centre of each mould on top of the jelly, then top up with the remaining mixture. Refrigerate for at least 5 hours (but best overnight). Serve with tropical fruits sprinkled with the reserved lime juice.

COOK'S TIPS
Serve straight from the refrigerator the day after it is made for best results. To loosen the jelly in its mould, place the mould in lukewarm water almost up to the rim for about 1 minute before turning it out. The jelly can also be made in a loaf terrine and cut into slices before serving.

COCKTAIL PARTIES

DEVILISH DRINKS SERVED IN ELEGANT GLASSES WITH PLATTERS OF DELECTABLE SAVOURIES, ALL AGAINST AN IMPRESSIVE BACKDROP OF HIGHLY POLISHED SILVERWARE, AND EXQUISITE FLOWERS: THESE ARE THE EXCITING ELEMENTS THAT MAKE UP THAT MOST GLAMOROUS OF OCCASIONS, THE COCKTAIL PARTY. THIS SHOULD NOT BE A TIME TO HOLD BACK: FOR A SENSATION-PACKED EVENT, MAKE SURE THAT YOU PULL OUT ALL THE STOPS.

Create a thrilling atmosphere with bold arrangements of flowers (right), wickedly indulgent drinks, and imaginative food from the cocktail menu (page 128).

GLAMOUR
"I can resist everything except temptation"

LIVELY PRESENTATION with a sophisticated atmosphere will guarantee that exotic delicacies and old-time favourites are both impossible to resist.

FLOWERS AND CANDLES

A low arrangement becomes even more effective when it includes candles. For safety, ensure the lit candles are taller than any plant material in the basket.

Ranunculus

Snapdragon

Tulip

Rose

Orchid

Ivy

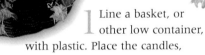

1 Line a basket, or other low container, with plastic. Place the candles, securing with adhesive putty. Fill the basket with soaked florists' foam, cutting it to fit round the candles. Place trailing foliage, such as ivy, round the edges.

2 Cut flower stems to 6cm (2½in). Insert them so they protrude about 2.5cm (1in) above the edge of the container. Arrange them in bands of colour, as the roses are here.

3 Keep the colour bands quite informal and fill in gaps with "pools" of flowers, hiding all the foam and plastic to complete the arrangement (above right).

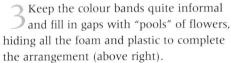

OSCAR WILDE 1854–1900

DRINKS TRAY
A polished silver tray reflects the glasses and their exciting contents, showing them off to great advantage.

BOLD PLATTER
Brilliant red plates echo the vibrant colours of some of the cocktail drinks, the food, and the basket of flowers.

COCKTAIL NAPKINS
When eating finger food, small napkins (linen for greatest luxury) are essential. Arrange a pile on the table within easy reach.

THE CHANCE TO IMPRESS

AN ELEGANT ARRANGEMENT

Flowers always play a key role in creating atmosphere, but they are especially important at cocktail or buffet parties where there is no formal seating plan. Position arrangements where they can be seen easily amidst your guests. Make use of side tables, cabinet tops, or wide mantlepieces and, in summer, place one or more arrangements on garden tables outdoors.

Astilbe

Rose

1 ◁ Wedge chicken wire or soaked florists' foam into a container. Insert stout-stemmed plants, such as the viburnum here, in a fan-like shape; make it balanced but not too formal.

2 ▷ Add the largest blooms, here highly scented white lilies, balancing them within the arrangement. Remove the pollen sacs that might stain guests' clothing.

3 ◁ Fill in with the remaining flowers: feathery white astilbe, ice blue delphiniums, and orange roses to tie in with the flower basket on pages 124-25. Then, assess the arrangement from a distance, inserting more material as necessary until you achieve the final effect (right).

Viburnum

FROSTED COCKTAILS

Merry Melon and Touch of the Blues, here, are just two of many colourful cocktails that will look most attractive with a salt or sugar edging on the glass. See pages 134–37 for drink recipes.

Delphinium

1 Mix 2–3 drops of natural food colouring into 4 tablespoons of caster sugar to produce a coloured edging. Moisten the rim of glass with lime juice or water and gently dip it into a plate of the sugar or table salt.

2 If the crystals on the rim are too large, clean the glass and begin again. Pour the cocktail carefully into the glass.

For a white edging use table salt or caster sugar

Lily

IMPORTANT ELEMENTS
Begin with a plant that has quite rigid stems to form the framework, add something bold to give balance, and then fill in with softer flowers.

A WINNING COMBINATION
The marriage of container and flowers is an important one. This display is shown off to perfection in the flowing silhouette of a Champagne cooler.

MENUS

"Cocktails are society's most enduring

COCKTAIL FOOD

~

These bite-sized delicacies are easy to eat: essential when
guests are standing, holding a glass, too. Serve the food from a tray
so cocktail sticks can be disposed of immediately and discreetly.

COCKTAIL KEBABS

*Tiny kebabs of prawns, scallops, artichokes,
asparagus, red pepper, mushrooms, and baby
corn, all wrapped in prosciutto and grilled.*

FILO PARCELS

*These miniature purses have a distinctly
North African flavour. Ricotta forms
the base for all three fillings:*
CHICKEN & APRICOT *with walnut.*
CURRANT & PINE NUT *with cinnamon.*
ARTICHOKE *with ginger and marjoram.*

FRUITS WITH PARMA HAM

*Firm but sweet chunks of papaya, mango,
fig, and melon are rolled up in delicate
strips of Parma ham.*

CROSTINI

*Crisp toasted baguette with a choice of
scrumptious toppings:*
MUSHROOM *cooked in red wine, with
pecans and nutmeg.*
MEDITERRANEAN *mix of tomatoes, olives,
capers, and herbs.*
TOMATO & BASIL, *a traditional combination
that never fails to please.*

SUSHI

*Bites of rice, fish, and vegetables that taste
as good as they look.*
SALMON BALLS, *smoked salmon encircles
delicate spheres of sushi rice.*
NORI ROLLS, *spirals of seaweed filled with
rice, vegetables, and fish.*
ROE BOATS, *seaweed-wrapped rice, topped
with caviar or lumpfish roe.*

PLANNING NOTES

The crostini toppings and the filo parcels can be cooked and frozen six weeks
ahead, or made and refrigerated the day before; the crostini bases are best fresh.
The sushi, the fruits in Parma ham, and the kebabs (up to their grilling) can be
prepared up to eight hours in advance and kept refrigerated. Cover the crostini
bases with topping, and heat these, the filo parcels, and the kebabs for six to
eight minutes in a moderate oven just before serving. The hot food is best fresh,
so enlist help in the kitchen if you can. *See pages 130–33 for recipes.*

invention" ELSA MAXWELL 1883-1963

COCKTAIL DRINKS

Beware, these rapturous alcoholic drinks, listed below
according to their base, are quite strong. Fortunately the non-
alcoholic punches are tempting and delicious, too.

TEQUILA
MARGARITA • FROZEN MARGARITA
MERRY MELON • TEQUILA SUNRISE

VODKA
BLACK & JADE • SEA BREEZE
VODKA MARTINI

WHISKY
WHISKY SOUR • SCOTCH MIST

BRANDY
MINT JULEP • SIDECAR

GIN
TOM COLLINS • PERFECT MARTINI
NEGRONI

RUM
PIÑA COLADA • DAIQUIRI
TOUCH OF THE BLUES • MY RUM PUNCH

CHAMPAGNE
CHAMPAGNE COCKTAIL • PIMM'S ROYAL
BLACK VELVET

NON-ALCOHOLIC PUNCHES
CRANBERRY • ORANGE
GRAPEFRUIT • APPLE

PLANNING NOTES
Select a maximum of three cocktails and two non-alcoholic punches for
your party; more than this will be difficult to manage, as the cocktails cannot
be mixed in advance. Making drinks for a crowd is a busy job: you will need a
full-time bartender for a large party. Equip your bartender with a cocktail
shaker, knives for cutting citrus fruits, a stirring spoon, and a strainer. Non-fizzy
bases for cocktails and punches can be made in advance, then shaken with ice
or mixed with the other chilled or fizzy ingredients. *See pages 134–37 for recipes.*

COCKTAIL FOOD 1

COCKTAIL KEBABS

⏱ 30 MINUTES   🍲 15 MINUTES   ▭ 1 HOUR SOAKING

INGREDIENTS FOR 24 KEBABS
12 MINIATURE ASPARAGUS SPEARS
4 BABY SWEET CORNS
½ RED PEPPER, CORED & DESEEDED
8 SLICES OF PROSCIUTTO, CUT VERY THIN
5 RAW TIGER PRAWNS, SHELLS REMOVED
5 BITE-SIZED SCALLOPS, CORALS REMOVED
24 COCKTAIL STICKS, SOAKED IN WATER
FOR 1 HOUR
60G (2 OZ) BUTTER, MELTED
6 BUTTON MUSHROOMS
3 ARTICHOKE HEARTS (BOTTLED OR CANNED),
HALVED

1 Preheat grill to medium. Cook the asparagus and the baby sweet corn in a saucepan of simmering, lightly salted water for 3–4 minutes, until *al dente*. Refresh in cold water, drain, then pat dry.

2 Cut the pepper into 6 long strips, about 1cm (½ in) thick.

3 Cut the prosciutto into 24 strips, about 12 x 2.5cm (5 x 1in), then use them to wrap individual sweet corns, prawns and scallops, securing each kebab with a cocktail stick. Brush with melted butter and grill for

about 2 minutes on each side, until the prawns have turned pink and the prosciutto just begins to brown.

4 Wrap three spears of asparagus in a piece of prosciutto and secure with a cocktail stick. Repeat to make 3 more kebabs. Brush with butter and grill for about 1 minute on each side, until the prosciutto begins to brown.

5 Wrap each mushroom in a strip of prosciutto and spear individually onto a cocktail stick with a piece of artichoke and a slice of pepper. Brush with melted butter and grill for about 3 minutes on each side until light brown.

COOK'S TIP
The kebabs can be cooked in advance, kept refrigerated, then heated in the oven at 180°C/350°F/Gas 4 for about 6 minutes before serving.

FRUITS WITH PARMA HAM

NOTES ON QUANTITIES
Allow up to eight canapés per person if you are serving them at a cocktail party, or three to five per person as pre-meal nibbles or a small starter. You may need fewer of the more filling ones, such as the crostini. The quantities for all recipes can be reduced or increased as necessary. The crostini bases, sushi rice, and filo pastry will provide enough for 72 canapés; reduce the amounts proportionally if you are making only one or two of the toppings or fillings. I would suggest preparing only one or two dishes for your party; the sushi, for instance, can be sufficient on its own.

FILO PARCELS

30 MINUTES ✦ 10 MINUTES

INGREDIENTS FOR **72** PARCELS
12 SHEETS FILO PASTRY, APPROXIMATELY
30 x 17CM (12 x 7IN)
90G (3OZ) BUTTER, MELTED
FILLING OF YOUR CHOICE (SEE BELOW)

1 Preheat oven to 190°C/375°F/Gas 5. Cut the filo pastry widthways into 3 sections, about 10cm (4in) wide, then halve each strip to make 72 squares.

2 Brush each square with melted butter and place 1½ teaspoons of the filling of your choice in the centre. Gather up the corners around the filling and twist them together to form a parcel.

3 Place on a greased baking sheet and bake for 8–10 minutes, until crisp and golden.

COOK'S TIPS
Preparation and cooking times refer only to the assembling and baking of the parcels. Keep filo pastry well wrapped or damp while using it. The parcels can be cooked and frozen for up to 6 weeks in advance. Defrost and heat in the oven at 180°C/350°F/Gas 4 for about 6 minutes.

CHICKEN & APRICOT

INGREDIENTS FOR **24** PARCELS
150G (5OZ) RICOTTA CHEESE
100G (3½ OZ) COOKED CHICKEN, FINELY CHOPPED
60G (2OZ) DRIED APRICOTS, FINELY CHOPPED
60G (2OZ) WALNUTS, TOASTED & FINELY CHOPPED
4 SPRING ONIONS, FINELY CHOPPED
2 TSP FRESH THYME, FINELY CHOPPED
SALT & PEPPER TO TASTE

Mix all the ingredients together in a large bowl.

CURRANT & PINE NUT

INGREDIENTS FOR **24** PARCELS
60G (2OZ) CURRANTS
90ML (3FL OZ) DRY WHITE WINE
150G (5OZ) RICOTTA CHEESE
60G (2OZ) PINE NUTS, TOASTED
½ TSP GROUND CINNAMON
SALT & PEPPER TO TASTE

Soak the currants in the wine overnight. Drain them well and mix them with the remainder of the ingredients.

ARTICHOKE

INGREDIENTS FOR **24** PARCELS
150G (5OZ) RICOTTA CHEESE
100G (3½ OZ) ARTICHOKE HEARTS (BOTTLED OR CANNED), FINELY CHOPPED
2 TSP FRESH MARJORAM, FINELY CHOPPED
4 SPRING ONIONS, FINELY CHOPPED
½ TSP GROUND GINGER
SALT & PEPPER TO TASTE

Mix all the ingredients together in a large bowl.

FRUITS WITH PARMA HAM

15 MINUTES

INGREDIENTS FOR **24** ITEMS
1 RIPE MANGO
½ SMALL MELON, DESEEDED
2 FIGS
12 THIN SLICES OF PARMA HAM, CUT IN HALF
24 COCKTAIL STICKS

1 Peel the mango and remove the flesh, cutting parallel to the flat side of the stone. Cut the flesh into 8 large chunks. Cut the melon flesh into 8 chunks, or scoop out 8 balls with a melon baller. Cut the figs into quarters.

2 Wrap a piece of Parma ham around each melon chunk and each piece of fig, securing it with a cocktail stick.

3 Secure a folded piece of ham on top of each mango chunk using a cocktail stick.

COOK'S TIPS
Other types of ham, such as prosciutto or Bayonne ham, and different fruits, like large strawberries or pear wedges, can also be used. This recipe can easily be doubled to make 48 wrapped fruits, or halved to make 12.

COCKTAIL FOOD 2

CROSTINI

 10 MINUTES   7 MINUTES

INGREDIENTS FOR 36 ITEMS
2 LARGE BAGUETTES, EACH CUT INTO 18 SLICES
1CM (½ IN) THICK
9 TBSP OLIVE OIL
2 GARLIC CLOVES (OPTIONAL)
SALT TO TASTE

1 Preheat oven to 220°C/425°F/Gas 7. Brush both sides of each slice of bread with oil, rub with garlic, if using, and sprinkle with salt.

2 Bake for 7 minutes until each slice is crisp and golden. Pile on your chosen topping, and serve immediately.

COOK'S TIPS
Preparation and cooking times refer to crisping the bases and adding the topping only. The bases are best eaten when fresh but the toppings can be frozen or made up to 8 hours ahead. Just before serving, cover the bases with topping and heat in the oven at 200°C/400°F/Gas 6 for 8 minutes, until crisp.

MUSHROOM

INGREDIENTS FOR 12 ITEMS
1 TBSP OLIVE OIL
250G (8OZ) SHITAKE MUSHROOMS, SLICED
200ML (7FL OZ) RED WINE
150ML (¼ PT) DOUBLE CREAM
¼ TSP GROUND NUTMEG
60G (2OZ) PECAN HALVES, LIGHTLY TOASTED

Heat the olive oil in a frying pan, add the mushrooms and cook for about 4 minutes, until they begin to soften. Add the red wine, then reduce until it has almost evaporated.

Stir in the cream, then reduce until it has all but disappeared. Remove from the heat and sprinkle on the nutmeg.

Spread on the crostini bases, prepared as above. Garnish with pecan halves.

MEDITERRANEAN

INGREDIENTS FOR 12 ITEMS
3 TBSP OLIVE OIL
90G (3OZ) SUN-DRIED TOMATOES, DRAINED & DICED
1 RED PEPPER, DESEEDED & CHOPPED
1 TBSP CAPERS, CHOPPED
1 GARLIC CLOVE, FINELY CHOPPED
1 TBSP FRESH OREGANO, FINELY CHOPPED, PLUS SPRIGS TO GARNISH
2 TSP BALSAMIC VINEGAR
1 TSP SUGAR
90G (3OZ) GREEN OLIVES, PITTED

Heat the olive oil in a frying pan, add the tomatoes, red pepper, capers, garlic, oregano, vinegar, sugar, and olives. Cook over a medium heat for 7 minutes.

Spread on the crostini bases, prepared as above. Garnish each slice with a sprig of oregano.

TOMATO & BASIL

INGREDIENTS FOR 12 ITEMS
500G (1LB) FRESH PLUM TOMATOES
1 TBSP OLIVE OIL
SALT TO TASTE
12 BASIL LEAVES, PLUS 4 TBSP FRESH BASIL, FINELY CHOPPED
2 TBSP PINE NUTS, LIGHTLY TOASTED

Preheat oven to 200°C/400°F/Gas 6. Cut the tomatoes in half lengthwise and place, cut side up, on greaseproof paper on a baking sheet. Brush the cut surfaces of the tomatoes with olive oil. Sprinkle with salt and bake for 1 hour.

Place a basil leaf on each crostini base, prepared as above, then a tomato half. Sprinkle with pine nuts and the chopped basil.

SUSHI

12 MINUTES   1 HOUR COOLING

INGREDIENTS FOR 72 ITEMS
425G (14OZ) PUDDING RICE
1 LITRE (1¾PT) WATER
200ML (7FL OZ) WHITE WINE VINEGAR
60G (2OZ) ICING SUGAR
8 GARLIC CLOVES, FINELY CHOPPED
4 X 5CM (2IN) PIECES OF FRESH ROOT GINGER,
FINELY CHOPPED
PINCH OF SALT

SUSHI
*Clockwise from
the top: Salmon
Balls, Nori Rolls,
and Roe Boats*

1 Place the rice and water in a large saucepan, cover, and bring to the boil. Simmer, keeping the pan covered, for about 12 minutes, until the rice has absorbed all the water and is sticky. If you cook half or a third of the rice it will still need 12 minutes cooking time.

2 Remove from the heat and immediately stir in the remaining ingredients. Leave to cool for at least 50 minutes. When cold, it is ready for shaping. Divide it into portions as required for the sushi recipes below.

COOK'S TIPS
If you do not wish to make all three types of sushi, divide it proportionately and cook. Cooking and cooling times refer to preparing only the rice.

SALMON BALLS

INGREDIENTS FOR 24 ITEMS
275G (9OZ) SMOKED SALMON, CUT INTO
24 X 8CM (3IN) SQUARES
300G (10OZ) SUSHI RICE
CHIVE LEAVES TO GARNISH

Lay a square of salmon onto a sheet of clingfilm. Place a small 2.5cm (1in) ball of rice, prepared as above, in the centre of the square and use the clingfilm to draw the salmon up round the ball. Screw the film up tightly to make a salmon-covered sphere. Repeat the process to make 24 balls. Refrigerate for about 4 hours, until firm, then remove the clingfilm. Decorate the tops with chives.

NORI ROLLS

INGREDIENTS FOR 24 ITEMS
4 SHEETS OF ROASTED SEAWEED SUSHI NORI
700G (1LB 7OZ) SUSHI RICE
125G (4OZ) VEGETABLES (SPRING ONIONS,
CHIVES, FINE GREEN BEANS, FINE STRIPS OF
COURGETTES, BABY CARROTS, OR PEPPERS)
250G (8OZ) FISH (COOKED PRAWNS, RED OR
BLACK ROE, FINE STRIPS OF SMOKED SALMON,
RAW TUNA, RAW SALMON, OR RAW SCALLOP)

Place a 20 x 18cm (8 x 7in) sheet of nori (shiny side down) onto a piece of clingfilm. Mist with water to soften. Spread a thin layer of rice, prepared as above, over the nori leaving a 2.5cm (1in) border along the two long edges.

Lay thin strips of vegetables and fish lengthways along one end of the rice. Mist the exposed nori edges and roll up lengthways, using the clingfilm to help you. Wrap the roll in the clingfilm and refrigerate for about 4 hours, until firm. Cut each roll into 6 slices, 2.5cm (1in) thick, then remove the clingfilm.

ROE BOATS

INGREDIENTS FOR 24 ITEMS
300G (10OZ) SUSHI RICE
4 SHEETS OF ROASTED SEAWEED SUSHI NORI,
EACH CUT INTO 6 STRIPS
6 TSP BLACK & RED ROE

Squeeze the rice, prepared as above, into 24 boat-shaped ovals, 2.5 x 1cm (1 x ½in). Mist the strips of nori then shape each one around a rice boat, pinching the ends together. Refrigerate for about 4 hours, until firm, then fill each boat with ¼ teaspoon of roe.

COCKTAIL DRINKS 1

TEQUILA BASE

FOR 1 GLASS

MARGARITA

1 SMALL LIME, JUICE ONLY
SALT
60ML (2FL OZ) TEQUILA
4 TSP TRIPLE SEC
ICE CUBES

Rub the rim of a cocktail glass with lime juice then dip in salt to give a fine coated rim. Shake the spirits and remaining lime juice with the ice then strain the liquid into the glass.

FROZEN MARGARITA

1 SMALL LIME, JUICE ONLY
SALT
60ML (2FL OZ) TEQUILA
4 TSP TRIPLE SEC
500ML (17FL OZ) ICE CUBES

Rub the rim of a cocktail glass with lime juice then dip in salt to give a fine coated rim. Place the ice in a blender. Pour in the spirits and remaining lime juice and blend for about 10 seconds until slushy. Scoop into the glass.

MERRY MELON

¼ SMALL MELON, DESEEDED
½ LEMON, JUICE ONLY
60ML (2FL OZ) TEQUILA
4 TSP GALLIANO
DROP VANILLA EXTRACT
ICE CUBES

In a food processor, pulp the melon flesh. Mix in the remaining ingredients. Shake with the ice for 15 seconds, then strain into a chilled cocktail glass.

TEQUILA SUNRISE

ICE CUBES
1 WEDGE OF LIME
60ML (2FL OZ) TEQUILA
1 ORANGE, JUICE ONLY
DASH OF GRENADINE
150ML (¼ PT) SODA WATER

Half fill a large highball glass with ice, squeeze the lime wedge over it and drop it in. Add the tequila, orange, and grenadine, and top up with soda.

BARTENDER'S NOTES

As cocktails are high in alcohol, I would allow only two or three drinks per person. You will need a bartender to prepare the drinks for 12 or more guests. Choose only two or three alcoholic cocktails and at least one soft punch. Where quantities make single drinks, multiply up for larger numbers. The basic ingredients, excluding ice and any fizzy drinks, can be mixed in advance and kept chilled. Shake or pour over ice and add any fizzy drinks when you serve.

MINT JULEP

SEA BREEZE

FROZEN MARGARITA

VODKA BASE
For 1 Glass

BLACK & JADE

50ML (2FL OZ) BLACKCURRANT VODKA
1 TSP CRÈME DE MURE OR CASSIS
1 TSP BLUE CURAÇAO
2 BLACKBERRIES OR 5 BLACKCURRANTS
ICE CUBES

Mix the spirits together. Place 2 blackberries or 5 blackcurrants in a chilled cocktail glass. Shake the liquid with ice for 15 seconds then pour it over the fruit.

SEA BREEZE

60ML (2FL OZ) VODKA
60ML (2FL OZ) GRAPEFRUIT JUICE
125ML (4FL OZ) CRANBERRY JUICE
ICE CUBES

Shake the vodka and fruit juices over the ice, then strain the liquid into a large highball glass.

VODKA MARTINI

1 TSP NOILLY PRAT, CHILLED
60ML (2FL OZ) VODKA, CHILLED
LEMON TWIST OR GREEN OLIVE

Pour the Noilly Prat into a chilled martini glass, twirl the glass to coat it, then pour the remainder back into the bottle. Swirl the vodka into the glass and add the lemon twist or olive.

WHISKY BASE
For 1 Glass

WHISKY SOUR

60ML (2FL OZ) BOURBON
½ TSP POWDERED SUGAR
½ LEMON, JUICE ONLY
2 MARASCHINO CHERRIES
ICE CUBES

Shake the bourbon, sugar, and lemon juice with the ice cubes and strain into a sour glass. Add the cherries.

SCOTCH MIST

60ML (2FL OZ) SCOTCH
30ML (1FL OZ) DRY VERMOUTH
½ TSP POWDERED SUGAR
1 EGG, ½ WHITE ONLY
ICE CUBES

Shake the Scotch, vermouth, sugar, and half an egg white with the ice cubes and strain into a cocktail glass.

BLACK
& JADE

BRANDY BASE
For 1 Glass

MINT JULEP

2 SUGAR CUBES
2 SPRIGS OF MINT
ICE CUBES, CRUSHED
60ML (2FL OZ) BRANDY OR BOURBON
3 TSP PEACH BRANDY

Rub the sugar cubes with mint leaves and place in a large highball glass. Half fill with ice then pour on the brandies. Stir well and top with a sprig of mint.

SIDECAR

60ML (2FL OZ) BRANDY
4 TSP TRIPLE SEC
½ LEMON, JUICE ONLY
ICE CUBES

Shake the spirits and lemon juice with ice cubes then strain into a chilled cocktail glass.

COCKTAIL DRINKS 2

GIN BASE

— For 1 Glass —

TOM COLLINS

ICE CUBES
60ML (2FL OZ) GIN
½ LEMON, JUICE ONLY
15G (½ OZ) SUGAR SYRUP
150ML (¼ PT) SODA WATER
TWIST OF LEMON
1 MARASCHINO CHERRY

Half fill a Collins glass with ice cubes. Stir in the gin, lemon juice, and sugar syrup. Top up with soda water, add the lemon, and decorate with a cherry.

PERFECT MARTINI

1 TSP NOILLY PRAT, CHILLED
60ML (2FL OZ) GIN, CHILLED
TWIST OF LEMON OR GREEN OLIVE

Pour the Noilly Prat into a chilled martini glass, twirl the glass to coat it, then return the rest to the bottle. Pour in the gin and add the twist of lemon.

NEGRONI

ICE CUBES
60ML (2FL OZ) GIN
3 TSP SWEET RED VERMOUTH
4 TSP CAMPARI
TWIST OF ORANGE

Half fill an aperitif glass with ice and stir in the gin, vermouth, and Campari. Add the twist of orange.

RUM BASE

— For 1 Glass —

PIÑA COLADA

100ML (3½ FL OZ) CRUSHED ICE
60ML (2FL OZ) PALE GOLDEN RUM
45ML (1½ FL OZ) COCONUT CREAM
90ML (3FL OZ) PINEAPPLE JUICE

Mix all the ingredients in a blender and pour into a Collins glass.

TOUCH OF THE BLUES

ICE CUBES
30ML (1FL OZ) WHITE RUM
2 TSP BLUE CURAÇAO
½ LIME, JUICE ONLY
2 TSP KIRSCH
PINCH OF GROUND NUTMEG

Shake all the liquid ingredients with the ice cubes then strain into a cocktail glass. Sprinkle with nutmeg.

DAIQUIRI

60ML (2FL OZ) PALE GOLDEN RUM
4 TSP LIME JUICE
1 TSP SUGAR SYRUP
ICE CUBES

Shake the rum, syrup, and lime with ice. Strain into a chilled cocktail glass.

MY RUM PUNCH

ICE CUBES
60ML (2FL OZ) GOLDEN RUM
1 LIME, JUICE ONLY
1 PASSION FRUIT, JUICE ONLY
150ML (¼ PT) PINEAPPLE JUICE, CHILLED
PINCH OF GROUND NUTMEG

Half fill a highball glass with ice and stir in the rum and fruit juices. Sprinkle with nutmeg.

PIÑA COLADA

PIMM'S ROYAL

CHAMPAGNE BASE
FOR 1 GLASS

CHAMPAGNE COCKTAIL

1 SUGAR CUBE
½ TSP ANGOSTURA BITTERS
250ML (8FL OZ) CHAMPAGNE
THIN WEDGE OF ORANGE
TWIST OF LEMON

Place the sugar cube at the bottom of a Champagne flute and shake on the Angostura bitters. Pour over the Champagne, then add the wedge of orange and the twist of lemon.

PIMM'S ROYAL

ICE CUBES
60ML (2FL OZ) PIMM'S NO 1
2 SLICES OF CUCUMBER
1 WEDGE OF LEMON
SPRIG OF MINT
175ML (6FL OZ) CHAMPAGNE, CHILLED

Half fill a large highball glass with ice cubes and pour over the Pimm's. Add the cucumber, wedge of lemon, and sprig of mint, then top up with chilled Champagne.

BLACK VELVET

125ML (4FL OZ) GUINNESS, CHILLED
125ML (4FL OZ) CHAMPAGNE, CHILLED

Pour the Guinness into a Champagne flute then top up with Champagne.

NON-ALCOHOLIC PUNCHES
FOR 24 GLASSES

CRANBERRY

3 LITRES (5PT) CRANBERRY JUICE
12 LEMONS, JUICE ONLY
1 LITRE (1¾PT) HIBISCUS TEA
2 LITRES (3PT) GINGER ALE, CHILLED

Mix the fruit juices and tea together and chill. Serve in highball glasses over ice, topped up with ginger ale.

ORANGE

2 LITRES (3PT) FRESH ORANGE JUICE
12 LIMES, JUICE ONLY
8 TSP ANGOSTURA BITTERS
4 LITRES (6PT) LEMONADE, CHILLED

Mix the fruit juices and bitters together and chill. Serve in highball glasses over ice, topped up with lemonade.

GRAPEFRUIT

2 LITRES (3PT) PINK GRAPEFRUIT JUICE
3 LITRES (5PT) LEMONADE
250ML (8FL OZ) ELDERFLOWER CORDIAL
12 LEMONS, JUICE ONLY
750ML (1¼ PT) GINGER ALE, CHILLED

Mix the first four ingredients together and chill. Serve in highball glasses over ice, topped up with ginger ale.

APPLE

3 LITRES (5PT) APPLE JUICE
12 LEMONS, JUICE ONLY
1 LITRE (1¾PT) PINEAPPLE JUICE
1 LITRE (1¾PT) SODA WATER, CHILLED

Mix the first three ingredients together and chill. Serve in highball glasses over ice, topped up with soda water.

BLACK VELVET

BARBECUES

FEW SENSATIONS SET OUR TASTE BUDS TINGLING LIKE THE WONDERFUL AROMA OF OUTDOOR COOKING AND THE UNIQUE FLAVOUR OF A BARBECUED MEAL. GLOWING WOOD AND COALS COOK MANY FOODS SUPERBLY. ADD TO THIS THE DELIGHT OF ALFRESCO LUNCHES ON WARM SUMMER DAYS OR EVENING ENTERTAINING UNDER A STARLIT SKY AND, LIKE ME, YOU WILL BE BARBECUING MORE AND MORE, SOMETIMES EVEN IN THE MIDDLE OF WINTER.

Enjoy the dishes of the Seafood Grill menu (page 144) by moon and lantern light (right). All fish and seafood cook extremely well on the barbecue.

MOONLIT
The smoky blue of a moonlit night cut up

MANY OF THE EVENING MEALS I remember most fondly are ones eaten outside, with flickering lanterns, the velvet night sky above, and enticing scents and flavours of food cooked over an aromatic wood fire.

SCENTED CANDLES

Frequently, the scented candles you buy have a rather synthetic perfume. A simple way to make your own for outside use is to drip five drops of essential oil onto the melted wax around the wick of a burning candle. Citronella and rosemary oil are good for deterring insects.

Use a pipette to drop in the oil

Take care not to drop oil on your hands

MARBLED LANTERNS

Cover the outside of jam or storage jars with marbled paper (page 70), and use them as sheltered candle holders.

1 On the back of a sheet of paper large enough to entirely encircle the jar, mark a line about 2.5cm (1in) above the jar's top.

3 Wrap the paper round the jar, attaching it to the glass with two-sided tape. Use a long taper to light the candle.

2 Cut out triangles from the top of the paper down to the line. Below the line, cut a pattern of moons and stars through which the light can shine.

Insert the candle first; anchor with putty if necessary

by sparkling stars

FLOWERS
The colours of this moonlit theme are echoed in the blue-green medley of ferns, delphinium, bells of Ireland, and euphorbia.

PAPER LANTERNS
For candlelight lanterns, make or buy marbelized paper in appropriate colours.

NAPKINS
Fold napkins into a triangle, then fold the top of the triangle over.

TUMBLER LIGHTS
Night-light candles in tumblers that shield them from evening breezes are both practical and appealing.

DAYTIME

Simple country food is best in the open air

MAKE SIMPLICITY your goal when setting the table for a lunchtime barbecue. Concentrate on comfort and relaxed informality.

INSTANT WINDOW BOX

Fill a wooden box with small potted plants and cut flowers. Use miniature roses in pots as the backbone, and fill in with cut flowers such as these anemones, sweet peas, and pittosporum.

FLOWER NAPKIN RING
Tuck a bold flower between each napkin and its ring. Choose blooms that do not wilt quickly.

1 Completely line a wooden box with plastic; a bin liner is ideal. Wrap and tape up the rose pots, too, to prevent their roots becoming waterlogged.

2 Place the pots in first, then wedge in soaked florists' foam, carved to fit around the plastic-covered pots. Trim overlapping plastic.

3 Insert the other flowers and foliage into the foam around the roses, keeping the stems fairly upright to simulate natural growth. Ensure the foam is hidden (see finished box above). To prolong the display, replace wilted flowers, and keep foam moist.

FINGER BOWL
A bowl of warm water with citrus slices for finger-dipping is a thoughtful gesture beside each setting at a barbecue.

JUG OF FLOWERS
Brighten up the table with a simple earthenware jug of flowers that echo the ones in the window box.

MENUS

A glowing, aromatic fire that perfumes food

SEAFOOD GRILL

Nothing beats the flavour of the freshest fish, cooked simply over a wood fire. *Serves 12*

CHARRED SQUID
Fragrant with a wild herb marinade, squid are always a delectable treat.

RED MULLET WITH FENNEL & ORANGE
Fennel enhances most white fish, and none better than the red mullet.

PEPPERED PINEAPPLE
Don't be alarmed by the idea of fruit and pepper. As with strawberries, the peppercorns intensify the fruit's flavour.

DRINKS
A crisp sharp Chablis has the strength to combine superbly with the nutty, smoky tastes of the fish. A Bourgogne Aligote would also complement the menu.

PLANNING NOTES
Mayonnaise for the mullet will keep for three days in the refrigerator. The marinade for the squid can be made the day before; allow up to four hours for the squid to marinate. Slice the pineapple and squeeze lemon over it to prevent discolouration up to two hours before serving. A second wire grill for your barbecue will save washing up between courses.
See pages 146–47 for recipes.

GOURMET BARBECUE

Don't cook only everyday food on a barbecue. Some of the best dishes I have ever eaten were prepared over wood fires. *Serves 6*

TEA-SMOKED TUNA
Sliced tuna, lightly smoked over tea leaves, is a delicacy to be savoured.

CRISPY CHICKEN LIVERS
Delicious chicken's liver, which is golden toasty crisp on the outside, and blush pink on the inside.

ROASTED PLANTAINS WITH RUM SAUCE
Ripe plantain, caramelized on the fire, with a sauce that transports you to the tropics.

DRINKS
I like to embrace a theme wholeheartedly, so as the food is smoky and quite special, a Pouilly Fumé would make a splendid fragrant accompaniment to this feast.

PLANNING NOTES
The sauce for the plantains can be prepared eight hours in advance, then reheated. Soak the chicken livers for two hours before you cook them. Grill the tuna first, serving it with a garnish of parsley and chervil, before barbecuing the livers.
See pages 148–49 for recipes.

and air

VEGETARIAN SPECIAL

The rich, earthy taste of mushrooms, tangy roasted goat's cheese, and seared polenta; every mouthful is ambrosia. *Serves 6*

SEARED GOAT'S CHEESE & TAPENADE
These two strong ingredients complement one another, particularly served on fragrant, herby focaccia.

MIXED MUSHROOM KEBABS
Mushrooms, artichokes, and shallots are roasted over charcoal for a richly flavoured trio.

PUMPKIN POLENTA
A northern Italian staple, enhanced with pumpkin and herbs, then seared on the grill.

DRINKS
A good Loire Sancerre or a New Zealand Sauvignon.

PLANNING NOTES
Tapenade will keep for one week, when stored in an airtight container. Make the mushroom marinade up to two days in advance, but do not marinate the kebabs for longer than 18 hours. Prepare the polenta to the end of step 4 the day before, to allow it to set. Its sauce can be made up to eight hours in advance, but do not add the cooked broccoli until the end. *See pages 150–51 for recipes.*

FEAST FOR A CROWD

These deliciously tender, marinated dishes are simple to prepare for large numbers of guests.
Serves 12

GINGER & GARLIC CHICKEN
Well-marinated, the chicken becomes mouthwateringly tender.

SEARED BEEF WITH THAI SAUCE
Do not be tempted to make this dish any spicier: it will detract from the flavour of the meat.

AROMATIC RICE SALAD
Tender rice, fragrant with spices and herbs.

DRINKS
Lightly warmed Saki, lager, or iced tea are the best refreshments for such spicy food.

PLANNING NOTES
Prepare the rice salad and the marinades for the chicken and the beef up to 12 hours in advance. Place the beef in to marinate immediately, but only marinate the chicken for up to 6 hours. The beef takes twice as long to cook as the chicken, so start cooking it 15 minutes before the chicken. *See pages 152–53 for recipes.*

SEAFOOD GRILL FOR 12

CHARRED SQUID

🗹 15 MINUTES · ⊔ 4 MINUTES · ☐ 4 HOURS MARINATING

INGREDIENTS
90ML (3FL OZ) OLIVE OIL
3 TBSP RED WINE VINEGAR
2 KIWI FRUITS, JUICE & PULP
4 GARLIC CLOVES, FINELY CHOPPED
4 SPRIGS FRESH ROSEMARY
12 SPRIGS FRESH MARJORAM
12 SQUID, PREPARED FOR COOKING
125G (4OZ) PLAIN FLOUR
1 TBSP DRIED MARJORAM

COOK'S TIP
Be very careful not to overcook the squid as it soon becomes tough.

1 To make the marinade, place the oil, vinegar, juice and pulp of the kiwi fruits, garlic, and herb sprigs in a non-metallic bowl.

2 Rinse the squid, dry well, and slice the sacs into 3 lengthwise.

3 Add the squid (sacs and small tentacles) to the marinade. Cover, and leave to marinate in the refrigerator for at least 4 hours.

4 Remove the squid, wiping off and reserving as much of the marinade as possible. Dip each piece into the flour and dried marjoram.

5 Baste the squid with the marinade and grill on the barbecue for about 2 minutes each side, until browned. Serve immediately.

CHARRED SQUID

NEW POTATO SALAD

RED MULLET WITH FENNEL & ORANGE

RED MULLET WITH FENNEL & ORANGE
30 MINUTES · 10 MINUTES

INGREDIENTS

1 LARGE WHOLE EGG (IF USING BLENDER)
OR 2 EGG YOLKS (IF WHISKING BY HAND)
2½ TSP DIJON MUSTARD
SALT & PEPPER TO TASTE
1 LEMON, JUICE ONLY
150ML (¼ PT) GRAPESEED OIL,
PLUS 3 TBSP FOR BASTING
150ML (¼ PT) OLIVE OIL
1 ORANGE, JUICE & GRATED ZEST
1 TBSP FENNEL SEEDS, GROUND
6 RED MULLET, FILLETED
NEW POTATO SALAD (SEE PAGE 186) AND
GREEN SALAD LEAVES TO SERVE

1 To make the mayonnaise, beat the whole egg or egg yolks, ½ teaspoon of mustard, and salt to taste until thickened. Stir in 1 tablespoon of lemon juice. Add a few drops of the grapeseed oil, stir well, and then add the remaining 150ml (¼ pint) in a slow, steady stream, beating constantly.

2 When all the grapeseed oil has been incorporated and the mixture has started to thicken, add the olive oil, very slowly, beating constantly until the mayonnaise is really thick. Season to taste.

3 Stir in the zest of the whole orange and the juice of half. Cover with clingfilm and refrigerate until needed.

4 In a small bowl, combine the juice of the remaining half orange, the fennel, the remaining mustard and 3 tablespoons of grapeseed oil. Baste the fish fillets with this mixture.

5 Grill the fillets for 3 minutes each side until the skin is golden and the flesh is no longer opaque. Serve with a dollop of mayonnaise, New Potato Salad, and green salad leaves.

COOK'S TIPS
Dried or fresh fennel stalks placed on the coals during grilling impart a wonderful flavour to the red mullet. Bay leaves (or leafy twigs) could also be used. The mayonnaise can be prepared in advance; it keeps in the refrigerator for 1 week.

PEPPERED PINEAPPLE
15 MINUTES · 12 MINUTES

INGREDIENTS

2 PINEAPPLES
60G (2OZ) UNSALTED BUTTER
1 LEMON, JUICE ONLY
1 TBSP GROUND BLACK PEPPER
250ML (8FL OZ) PINEAPPLE JUICE
1 LIME, JUICE ONLY
2 TSP ORANGE FLOWER WATER

1 Cut the top and bottom off the pineapples and peel. Cut each pineapple into 6 wedges. Remove the tough central cores, and cut grooves along the width to remove the eyes.

2 Rub butter and lemon juice all over the pineapple wedges, and sprinkle with coarse pepper.

3 To make the sauce, heat the pineapple and lime juices in a saucepan and boil until reduced by half. Stir in the orange flower water.

4 Grill the pineapple for about 6 minutes each side, until golden. Pour over the fruit juices and serve.

COOK'S TIP
Increase or decrease the number of slices of pineapple according to the size of your party. Increase the sauce proportionately, but do not reduce it by more than half.

GOURMET BARBECUE FOR 6

TEA-SMOKED TUNA

10 MINUTES   10 MINUTES

INGREDIENTS
1.25KG (2½LB) TUNA, IN 6 X 1CM (½IN) STEAKS
SALT & PEPPER TO TASTE
4 TBSP OLIVE OIL
2 TBSP EACH LAPSANG SOUCHONG TEA LEAVES
& GREEN OR CHINA TEA LEAVES
4 TBSP SOFT BROWN SUGAR
MARJORAM SPRIGS TO GARNISH

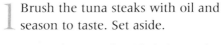

1 Brush the tuna steaks with oil and season to taste. Set aside.

2 Line a large wok with foil. Combine the teas and sugar and place inside the wok on the foil.

3 When the barbecue is very hot, cover the wok and place over the flame. When the tea mixture begins to smoke, place a wire rack inside the wok, and lay as many slices of tuna on the rack as it will hold.

4 Cook for about 5 minutes, turning halfway through cooking, until the tuna is pale brown on the outside but still pink in the middle, then remove and keep warm. Repeat with the remaining tuna, using the same tea mixture. Garnish with marjoram sprigs and serve with green salad leaves.

COOK'S TIP
Take care not to oversmoke the tuna, as you risk overwhelming the flavour of the fish.

CRISPY CHICKEN LIVERS

10 MINUTES   10 MINUTES   2 HOURS SOAKING

INGREDIENTS
750G (1½LB) CHICKEN LIVERS
150ML (¼PT) MILK
2 TBSP WHITE WINE VINEGAR
100G (3½OZ) FRESH WHITE BREADCRUMBS
1 TBSP FRESH THYME, FINELY CHOPPED
SALT & PEPPER TO TASTE
6 TBSP DIJON MUSTARD
4 TBSP OLIVE OIL
GREEN SALAD LEAVES TO SERVE

1 Rinse the chicken livers and remove any white sinew. Place them in a bowl and cover with the milk and vinegar. Leave to soak for at least 2 hours.

2 Just before cooking, drain the livers and pat dry with kitchen paper. Discard the milk and vinegar.

3 Combine the breadcrumbs, thyme, and seasoning. Coat the livers in the mustard, roll them in the breadcrumb mixture, and dab with oil.

4 Place the chicken livers on a greased wire rack on the barbecue and cook for about 5 minutes each side, dabbing with extra oil if necessary, until they are crispy on the outside and slightly pink inside. Serve immediately on a bed of green salad leaves.

COOK'S TIP
For the best results, cook these on the barbecue while the coals are still very hot. Place the livers at medium height above the coals.

ROASTED PLANTAINS WITH RUM SAUCE

10 MINUTES   7 MINUTES

INGREDIENTS
6 RIPE (ALMOST BLACK) SWEET PLANTAINS
3 LIMES, JUICE ONLY
2 TBSP DARK RUM
60G (2OZ) UNSALTED BUTTER
4 TBSP SOFT BROWN SUGAR
SINGLE CREAM OR ICE CREAM TO SERVE

1 Cut the plantains in half lengthwise. Brush the cut side with the juice of 1 lime, and roast on the barbecue, skin side down, for 3 minutes.

2 While the plantains are cooking, in a small saucepan heat the rum, half the butter, the remaining lime juice, and the sugar, until the sugar has dissolved. Remove from the heat.

3 Brush the cut sides of the plantains with the remaining butter and turn over, cut side to the flame. Roast for a further 3–4 minutes, until dark golden. Pour the sauce over the plantains and serve with single cream or ice cream.

COOK'S TIPS
If plantains are unavailable, large bananas are also delicious cooked in this way. The sauce can be made a day in advance and reheated.

ROASTED PLANTAINS WITH RUM SAUCE

VEGETARIAN SPECIAL FOR 6

SEARED GOAT'S CHEESE & TAPENADE

⏱ 10 MINUTES 🍲 4 MINUTES

INGREDIENTS
250G (8OZ) BLACK OLIVES, PITTED
60G (2OZ) CAPERS
5 FRESH SAGE LEAVES
2 GARLIC CLOVES, COARSELY CHOPPED
90ML (3FL OZ) OLIVE OIL
2 TSP BALSAMIC VINEGAR
½ LEMON, JUICE & GRATED ZEST
6 SMALL GOAT'S CHEESES
GREEN SALAD LEAVES, WALNUT DRESSING
(SEE PAGE 185) & FOCACCIA (SEE PAGE 186)
TO SERVE

1 To make the tapenade, blend together all the ingredients (except the cheese) in a food processor to a smooth but slightly grainy paste.

2 Divide the cheeses horizontally in half and grill skin side down for 2 minutes, until they just begin to melt.

3 Serve the seared goat's cheese on a bed of green salad leaves with Walnut Dressing, a spoonful of tapenade, and Focaccia. Break the bread into chunks, and sear over the barbecue for about 2 minutes on each side before serving.

COOK'S TIP
Watch the cheese carefully while grilling: do not allow it to melt and drip over the coals.

SEARED GOAT'S
CHEESE

FOCACCIA

TAPENADE

MIXED MUSHROOM KEBABS

—— 🥄 55 MINUTES 🍲 35 MINUTES ⬜ 2 HOURS MARINATING ——

INGREDIENTS

4 SHALLOTS, FINELY CHOPPED, PLUS 24 WHOLE
SHALLOTS, UNPEELED
2 TBSP FRESH SAGE, FINELY CHOPPED, PLUS 12
WHOLE SAGE LEAVES
3 GARLIC CLOVES, CRUSHED
125ML (4FL OZ) OLIVE OIL, PLUS EXTRA FOR
BASTING
625G (1¼LB) MIXED MUSHROOMS
400G (13OZ) ARTICHOKE HEARTS (CANNED
OR BOTTLED), HALVED
12 WOODEN BARBECUE STICKS
PUMPKIN POLENTA (SEE BELOW) TO SERVE

1 To make the marinade, place the chopped shallots, chopped sage, garlic, and olive oil in a non-metallic bowl. Prepare the mushrooms (see Step 1, page 96) and add to the marinade. Stir gently. Cover and leave to marinate in the refrigerator for 2–18 hours, turning occasionally.

2 Soak the wooden sticks in water for 30 minutes. Meanwhile, grill the whole shallots on the barbecue for 30 minutes, until just cooked, then peel.

3 Thread the mushrooms and shallots onto the sticks with the whole sage leaves and artichokes. Dab with a little oil and grill for 5 minutes per side, basting with the oil occasionally during cooking, until golden and tender. Serve with a green leaf salad and Pumpkin Polenta.

PUMPKIN POLENTA

—— 🥄 35 MINUTES 🍲 1 HOUR 15 MINUTES ⬜ 12 HOURS SETTING ——

INGREDIENTS

125ML (4FL OZ) OLIVE OIL
5 GARLIC CLOVES, FINELY CHOPPED
375G (12OZ) PUMPKIN FLESH, COARSELY
CHOPPED
SALT & PEPPER TO TASTE
1.5 LITRES (2½PT) WATER
2 TSP SALT
375G (12OZ) PRE-COOKED INSTANT POLENTA
3½ TBSP FRESH OREGANO, FINELY CHOPPED
1½ TSP GROUND BLACK PEPPER
125G (4OZ) BUTTER
2 ONIONS, FINELY CHOPPED
500G (1LB) TOMATOES, SKINNED & CHOPPED
1 TBSP TOMATO PURÉE
250ML (8FL OZ) VEGETABLE STOCK
(SEE PAGE 185)
375G (12OZ) BROCCOLI, CUT INTO SMALL
FLORETS & TENDER STEMS DICED
90G (3OZ) PARMESAN CHEESE, GRATED

1 Heat 2 tablespoons of the oil in a saucepan, add 2 garlic cloves and the pumpkin and fry gently for about 5 minutes, until dark golden. Cover the pumpkin with lightly salted water, and simmer, covered, for 20 minutes. Drain and mash half of the pumpkin. Reserve the other half for the sauce.

2 To make the polenta, fill a large saucepan with 1.5 litres (2½ pints) water, add the 2 teaspoons of salt, and bring to the boil. Put the polenta into a jug and pour it into the pan in a steady stream, beating constantly to prevent lumps forming.

3 Add 1½ tablespoons of oregano and pepper, then turn down the heat to the lowest setting. Cook for 10 minutes, stirring constantly, until the spoon can stand up in the mixture. As soon as the polenta is ready, stir in the mashed pumpkin and butter.

4 Spoon the polenta into a greased 30cm (12in) square tin and leave, covered, overnight to set.

5 Make the sauce: heat 2 tablespoons of the oil in a saucepan and gently fry the onions and remaining garlic for about 10 minutes, stirring, until pale golden and softened.

6 Add the tomatoes, tomato purée, remaining oregano, and stock. Season, and cook for about 10 minutes, until the sauce has reduced to a liquid pulp. Stir in the broccoli and remaining pumpkin pieces, cover, and cook for 4 minutes, until the broccoli is *al dente*.

7 Cut the set polenta into 24 slices, brush with the remaining olive oil and grill for about 8 minutes each side, until golden. Sprinkle with the Parmesan and serve hot with the sauce and the Mixed Mushroom Kebabs.

FEAST FOR A CROWD FOR 12

GINGER & GARLIC CHICKEN

10 MINUTES · 25 MINUTES · 2 HOURS MARINATING

INGREDIENTS
1 LITRE (1¾ PT) LIVE NATURAL YOGURT
5 LIMES (JUICE & GRATED ZEST OF 3, PLUS
2 CUT INTO WEDGES TO GARNISH)
7CM (3IN) PIECE OF FRESH GINGER, PEELED
& CUT INTO THIRDS
1 TBSP EACH GROUND CUMIN, FENUGREEK
& TURMERIC
3 GARLIC CLOVES, CRUSHED
1 FRESH RED CHILLI, DESEEDED &
FINELY CHOPPED
3 SHALLOTS, FINELY CHOPPED
12 CHICKEN BREASTS, ABOUT 2KG
(4LB), BONED & SKINNED
AROMATIC RICE SALAD (SEE
OPPOSITE) TO SERVE

1 To make the marinade, blend all the ingredients (except the chicken, lime wedges, and rice salad) in a food processor, until smooth.

2 Place the chicken breasts in a single layer in a large non-metallic dish and prick lightly with a fork all over.

Spoon the marinade over the chicken. Cover and leave to marinate in the refrigerator for 2–6 hours.

3 Remove the chicken and shake off as much marinade as possible, reserving 150ml (¼ pint) for the Aromatic Rice Salad. Grill for about 8 minutes each side, until it is golden and tender. Garnish with lime wedges and serve with Aromatic Rice Salad and a red leaf salad.

AROMATIC
RICE SALAD

GINGER & GARLIC
CHICKEN

SEARED BEEF WITH THAI SAUCE

25 MINUTES 30 MINUTES 4 HOURS MARINATING

INGREDIENTS

7 GARLIC CLOVES, CRUSHED
7 FRESH RED CHILLIES, DESEEDED & FINELY CHOPPED
5 LIMES, JUICE & GRATED ZEST
1.5KG (3LB) BEEF SIRLOIN OR ENTRECÔTE
125ML (4FL OZ) WATER
5 TBSP WHITE WINE VINEGAR
6 ANCHOVY FILLETS, MASHED
2 SHALLOTS, FINELY CHOPPED
2½ TBSP FISH SAUCE
1 TBSP CASTER SUGAR
AROMATIC RICE SALAD (SEE BELOW) TO SERVE

1 To make the marinade, mix together 4 garlic cloves, 4 chillies, and the juice and zest of 3 limes.

2 Place the beef in a non-metallic dish and pour over the marinade. Cover and leave to marinate in the refrigerator for about 4 hours, turning the beef over half way through.

3 To make the sauce, combine the water, vinegar, anchovies, shallots, fish sauce, caster sugar, and the remaining garlic, chillies, and lime juice and zest. Cover with clingfilm and refrigerate until needed.

4 Remove the beef from the refrigerator and shake off as much marinade as possible. Transfer to the barbecue and grill for about 15 minutes each side, basting with the marinade halfway through cooking, until the meat is golden on the outside but still pink in the middle.

5 Leave the beef to rest in a warm place for 5 minutes, then carve it into thin slices. Pour over the sauce. Serve with Aromatic Rice Salad.

AROMATIC RICE SALAD

10 MINUTES 15 MINUTES 30 MINUTES SOAKING

INGREDIENTS

1KG (2LB) BASMATI RICE
4 TBSP GROUNDNUT OIL
30G (1OZ) BUTTER
20 CARDAMOMS, SEEDS CRUSHED
750ML (1¼PT) WATER
150ML (¼PT) RESERVED MARINADE (SEE STEP 3 OPPOSITE)
1 ORANGE PEPPER, DESEEDED & CUT INTO SMALL, THIN STRIPS
3 TSP SALT
GINGER & GARLIC CHICKEN (SEE OPPOSITE) TO SERVE

1 Wash the rice in a sieve under running water until the water runs clear. Soak for 30 minutes then drain thoroughly for 5.

2 Heat the oil and butter in a large saucepan over a moderate heat until the butter just begins to brown. Immediately add the rice and the cardamom seeds, stirring until they are well coated. Cook for about 2 minutes, then add the water, marinade, pepper slices, and salt.

3 Bring to the boil, turn the heat down to very low, and cover. Cook for 9 minutes, then remove from the heat, stir, fluff up with a fork, and allow to cool in the covered pan. Serve hot or cold, with Ginger & Garlic Chicken and a mixed salad.

153

PICNICS

INVITE YOUR FRIENDS TO JOIN YOU FOR A PICNIC IN THE COUNTRYSIDE OR BY THE SEA. UNPACK THE HAMPERS, AND SAVOUR THE LUXURIOUS LANGUOR OF A PROTRACTED OUTDOOR MEAL. COMBINE SIMPLE BUT SPECIAL RUSTIC FLAVOURS OF GOOD FOOD WITH CHILLED WHITE WINE, BEER, OR FRESH FRUIT JUICE. PICNICS ARE A WONDERFUL WAY TO CREATE A SMALL PATCH OF PARADISE, LEAVING A FEELING OF RELAXATION AND RENEWAL, A SENSE OF HAVING TAKEN A HOLIDAY.

Once you and your guests are replete with Herbed Country Pâté and Parslied Ham from the Country Hamper menu (page 158), lie back and enjoy the sky (right).

SUMMER

Lazy, hazy summer days of meals, to the

ONE OF THE BEST aspects of picnics is that the work is done in advance, leaving you free to concentrate on setting up, serving, and enjoying the occasion itself.

TABLECLOTH
If you are picnicking on the ground, spread a small cloth on a larger undercloth to keep the food well clear of sand or dirt.

PACKING FOR A PICNIC

Wrap plates and cutlery in decorative cotton napkins and tea towels, and transport in large wicker baskets. Pack the food and drink in cake tins and cooler bags.

1 Fold a cotton napkin in half. Place a set of cutlery pointing from top left towards the middle, and start to wrap the napkin loosely around it.

2 Roll the napkin in a slight semi-circle to form a cone. Secure it about two-thirds of the way down by tying several strands of raffia firmly around the cutlery in a bow.

3 Arrange the napkin rolls in a box in a basket with other non-food items, packed firmly to prevent breakages. Use the picnic cloth to protect fragile items, or to shield the food from direct sunlight.

YELLOW & BLUE
Keep to an informal colour scheme, and don't worry if items don't match exactly.

sound of waves or rustling leaves

SEA SHELLS
Decorate your picnic table with elements from the surrounding area: a plate of shells, for example, for a seaside picnic.

CUTLERY BASKET
A square box, centrally placed for accessibility, holds the wrapped cutlery for each guest. Use the box to keep it together after the meal.

HERB BUNCHES
Make small posies of herbs for all your guests. They can take them home after the picnic and hang them up to dry out.

MENUS
To eat under the skies is bliss

COUNTRY HAMPER

No-one will go hungry after sampling soda bread,
ham cooked with parsley, and a coarse herby pâté.
Serves 12

RAISIN & OREGANO SODA BREAD
*Quick and easy to make, it is almost impossible to resist
eating this bread as it comes out of the oven.*

PARSLIED HAM
*Ham and vegetables set in a tangy stock is a traditional
Easter dish in France.*

HERBED COUNTRY PÂTÉ
*Made from pork and chicken, this pâté looks and tastes
wonderfully wholesome.*

DRINKS
*Choose a Bourgogne Aligote, served chilled, to partner
this picnic. If you would prefer a red wine, Merlot is a
good alternative.*

PLANNING NOTES
The parslied ham improves with time: ideally prepare it
three days in advance, but at least a day before eating. Both
the ham and the pâté will keep for one week, covered, in the
refrigerator. The bread is best when freshly made, but can be
frozen for up to six weeks. *See pages 160–61 for recipes.*

FRENCH PICNIC

Two dishes from the south of France, and an
upside-down tart, make this an appealing menu
for a late summer picnic. *Serves 6*

PISSALADIÈRE
Enjoy this French "pizza" hot or cold.

SALAD NIÇOISE
A hearty salad packed with the flavours of the sun.

QUINCE TART TATIN
*Quince are wonderfully perfumed, but both apples and pears
are good alternatives in this upside-down tart.*

DRINKS
*As the picnic has a French flavour, choose French wine:
a white Bordeaux or a good rosé from the south.*

PLANNING NOTES
Enjoy the pissaladière fresh, up to 24 hours after it is made,
or freeze it for a maximum of six weeks; it is delicious hot or
cold. The salad must be prepared on the day, and dressed at
the last moment. The tart is best eaten within a day of being
made. *See pages 162–63 for recipes.*

EXOTIC SPREAD

Asian food may not be the first thing that comes to mind for a picnic, but this spicy feast is well worth trying. *Serves 12*

SPICY CHICKEN WITH PAPAYA SALAD
Ginger and garlic are predominant flavours in this dish, balanced by the wonderfully fresh-tasting papaya salad.

SPICY LAMB KEBABS
Skewered pieces of lamb are meltingly tender, with a sweet-sour chilli and cumin sauce.

INDIAN MILK PUDDING
This creamy rice pudding with a burnt-sugar topping slices easily: perfect for a picnic.

DRINKS
Cold lager, preferably Indian Kingfisher Lager, is the best alcohol to accompany these tangy dishes. Chilled sparkling water with slices of lime is also refreshing.

PLANNING NOTES
The milk pudding will keep for four to five days in the refrigerator, but it is best to grill the sugar topping the morning before eating. Both the meat dishes improve with time, and can be kept for one or two days in the refrigerator. *See pages 164–65 for recipes.*

DINE IN STYLE

These dishes are ideal for an elegant picnic, perhaps for an outdoor concert, the races, or for a celebratory meal somewhere special. *Serves 6*

DUCK & ROCKET SALAD
Duck, marinated in sherry vinegar and cooked with olives and rosemary, is served thinly sliced on a bed of rocket.

FENNEL & CHEESE TART
These two flavours complement each other so well; combine them in an easy-to-eat tart.

POLENTA CAKE
Serve small slices of this rich-textured cake: there will be plenty left for second helpings later in the day.

DRINKS
Full-bodied Californian Zinfandel or Italian Amarone della Valpollicella would suit both the duck and the tart. Follow with a moderately sweet Vin Santo from Tuscany to enjoy with the polenta cake.

PLANNING NOTES
All three dishes can be made 24 hours in advance, although the salad should be assembled at the last minute. Refrigerate the duck in an airtight container, either whole or cut into slices to stop it drying out. Store the cake upside down in a cake tin so its base sits on the lid; this makes it easy to cut without transferring it to a plate. *See pages 166–67 for recipes.*

COUNTRY HAMPER FOR 12

RAISIN & OREGANO SODA BREAD

☑ 15 MINUTES 🍲 40 MINUTES

INGREDIENTS
300G (10OZ) PLAIN WHOLEMEAL FLOUR
300G (10OZ) PLAIN FLOUR
1 TSP BICARBONATE OF SODA
2 TSP BAKING POWDER
2 TBSP CASTER SUGAR
1 TSP SALT
1 LARGE EGG
90ML (3FL OZ) MILK
350ML (12FL OZ) LIVE NATURAL YOGURT
125G (4OZ) RAISINS
2 TSP FRESH OREGANO, FINELY CHOPPED

COOK'S TIP
To test if the bread is done, turn the loaf over and tap the base with your knuckles. If it sounds hollow, it is ready.

1 Preheat oven to 190°C/375°F/Gas 5. In a large mixing bowl, sift both types of flour, the bicarbonate of soda, baking powder, sugar, and salt.

2 Lightly beat the egg, milk, and yogurt, and add to the mixing bowl, together with the raisins and oregano.

3 With your hand, draw the flour into the yogurt mixture to make a soft, sticky dough. On a floured work surface, knead the dough for about 2 minutes, then shape it into a round loaf, about 5cm (2in) high.

4 With floured hands, transfer the loaf to a lined baking sheet, cut a cross 5mm (¼in) deep in the centre, and bake for 40 minutes, until it is brown. Remove from the oven, and transfer to a wire rack to cool.

CELERIAC
RÉMOULADE

HERBED
COUNTRY
PÂTÉ

PARSLIED HAM

160

PARSLIED HAM

✓ 25 MINUTES ⌾ 2 HOURS 50 MINUTES ☐ 24 HOURS SOAKING PLUS 12 HOURS CHILLING

INGREDIENTS

2.5KG (5LB) UNCOOKED GAMMON OR BOILING
HAM, SOAKED FOR 24 HOURS
750ML (1¼PT) DRY WHITE WINE
12 SHALLOTS, PEELED & HALVED
6 CARROTS, CUT INTO LARGE ROUNDS
2 CELERY STICKS, CUT INTO LARGE SLICES
2 GARLIC CLOVES, PEELED & HALVED
3 BAY LEAVES
2 SPRIGS EACH FRESH ROSEMARY & TARRAGON
4 SPRIGS FRESH SAGE
6 SPRIGS FRESH THYME
1 TBSP GREEN PEPPERCORNS
2½ TBSP POWDERED GELATINE
90ML (3FL OZ) WATER
5 TBSP TARRAGON OR WHITE WINE VINEGAR
90ML (3FL OZ) BRANDY (OPTIONAL)
150G (5OZ) FRESH FLAT-LEAF PARSLEY, FINELY
CHOPPED, PLUS 12 SPRIGS TO GARNISH
CELERIAC RÉMOULADE (SEE PAGE 187) TO SERVE

1 Rinse the pre-soaked ham and place it in a large saucepan with the wine, shallots, carrots, celery, garlic, bay leaves, rosemary, tarragon, sage, thyme, and peppercorns. Pour over enough water to completely cover the ham, bring to the boil, and simmer for 2 hours 30 minutes, until well done. Allow to cool.

2 Remove the ham and strain the stock, reserving the vegetables. Bring the stock to the boil, and reduce to 1 litre (1¾ pints).

3 Meanwhile, sprinkle the gelatine onto the water in a small saucepan. Leave to soak for 5 minutes. Warm over a very low heat until the gelatine has dissolved and the liquid is clear.

Add the vinegar and brandy, if using, to the simmering stock, then whisk in the gelatine. Taste and adjust seasoning. Allow the stock to cool for 2–3 hours, until it nears setting point.

4 While the stock is cooling, trim the ham of skin and fat and cut it into both large and small chunks. In alternating layers, arrange the meat, vegetables, and chopped parsley in a 2 litre (3 pint) deep oval bowl or terrine. Pour over the stock just before it sets. Cover with clingfilm and refrigerate for at least 12 hours. Garnish with parsley and serve with Celeriac Rémoulade.

COOK'S TIPS

This is best made 3 days in advance. Carry to the picnic in a chill box and serve from the bowl.

HERBED COUNTRY PÂTÉ

✓ 20 MINUTES ⌾ 2 HOURS 15 MINUTES ☐ 24 HOURS MARINATING

INGREDIENTS

90ML (3FL OZ) MEDIUM SHERRY
90ML (3FL OZ) BRANDY
3 GARLIC CLOVES, CRUSHED
3 BAY LEAVES, PLUS 6 TO GARNISH
1 TBSP FRESH TARRAGON, FINELY CHOPPED
1 TSP SALT
½ TSP GROUND WHITE PEPPER
625G (1¼LB) CHICKEN LIVERS, CUT INTO
1CM (½IN) CUBES
300G (10OZ) BELLY OF PORK, SKINNED, CUT
INTO 1CM (½IN) CUBES
250G (8OZ) MINCED PORK
250G (8OZ) SMOKED STREAKY BACON,
DERINDED
3 CHICKEN BREASTS, BONED & SKINNED, CUT
INTO 5 X 2CM (2 X ¾IN) STRIPS
6 PICKLED GHERKINS, QUARTERED LENGTHWISE

1 To make the marinade, combine the sherry, brandy, garlic, 3 bay leaves, tarragon, and seasoning in a large, non-metallic bowl.

2 Add the chicken livers, belly of pork, and minced pork. Cover, and leave to marinate in the refrigerator for 24 hours, turning occasionally. Discard the bay leaves.

3 Preheat oven to 200°C/400°F/Gas 6. Grease a 23 x 12cm (9 x 5in) terrine or loaf tin and line the base and sides with bacon strips, stretching them over the back of a knife if necessary. Leave them hanging over the edge of the terrine. Set the remaining bacon aside.

4 In the terrine, place one-third of the marinated meat, followed by one-third of the marinade, then the chicken. Repeat, adding the gherkins instead of the chicken. Finally, spoon over the remaining meat and marinade.

5 Fold over the bacon, lay the reserved slices on top, and decorate the surface with 6 bay leaves. Cover with foil. Place in a roasting tin filled with boiling water and cook for 2 hours 15 minutes. Serve cold with Raisin & Oregano Soda Bread (see opposite).

COOK'S TIPS

This pâté is best made a few days in advance. It will keep for 1 week in the refrigerator.

FRENCH PICNIC FOR 6

PISSALADIÈRE

🥄 30 MINUTES 🍲 45 MINUTES

INGREDIENTS
375G (12OZ) PUFF PASTRY (SEE PAGE 184)
2 TBSP OLIVE OIL
750G (1½LB) ONIONS, THINLY SLICED
4 GARLIC CLOVES, CRUSHED
750G (1½LB) FRESH PLUM TOMATOES,
SKINNED, DESEEDED & COARSELY CHOPPED
2 TBSP TOMATO PURÉE
2 TSP CASTER SUGAR
2 TBSP FRESH MARJORAM, FINELY CHOPPED,
PLUS 10 SPRIGS TO GARNISH
10 ANCHOVY FILLETS, HALVED LENGTHWISE
SALT & PEPPER TO TASTE
1 EGG, YOLK ONLY
1 TSP MILK
30 BLACK OLIVES, PITTED

1 For the crust, roll out the pastry into a 32cm (13in) circle, then cut a 2cm (1in) strip from around the outside. Brush the strip with water and lay it over the edge of the 30cm (12in) circle to form a rim made from a double layer of pastry.

2 Make a criss-cross pattern around the rim with a knife. Prick the base of the tart all over with a fork. Refrigerate for 30 minutes.

3 Meanwhile, prepare the filling. Preheat oven to 200°C/400°F/Gas 6. Heat the olive oil in a saucepan and cook the onions and garlic, covered, for about 18 minutes, stirring from time to time, until softened. Add the tomatoes, tomato purée, sugar, and chopped marjoram and cook for about 5 minutes over a medium heat, stirring occasionally, to make a thick purée.

4 Spread the onion mixture over the pastry base. Arrange the marjoram sprigs and anchovies on top, radiating out from the centre. Sprinkle with salt and pepper, and brush the edge of the tart with the egg yolk mixed with milk.

5 Bake for 20–25 minutes, until the pastry has puffed around the edges. Remove from the oven and decorate with the olives.

PISSALADIÈRE

SALAD NIÇOISE

⏱ 20 MINUTES 🍲 25 MINUTES

INGREDIENTS

24 SMALL NEW POTATOES, ABOUT
500G (12OZ), SCRUBBED
250G (8OZ) FRENCH BEANS
150G (5OZ) FRESH PEAS
3 EGGS
500G (1LB) FRESH OR CANNED TUNA
12 ANCHOVY FILLETS
6 TOMATOES, CUT INTO WEDGES
100G (3½OZ) BLACK OLIVES, UNPITTED
6 SPRING ONIONS, THINLY SLICED LENGTHWISE
HALF A CUCUMBER, THINLY SLICED
1 FENNEL BULB, THINLY SLICED
18 RADISHES
GREEN SALAD LEAVES
2 TSP EACH OF FRESH HERBS, FINELY CHOPPED:
THYME, OREGANO, MARJORAM, MINT
3 TBSP FRESH BASIL, SHREDDED
175ML (6FL OZ) VINAIGRETTE (SEE PAGE 185)

1 In a saucepan of salted boiling water, cook the potatoes for about 15 minutes, or until soft. When cool, slice them in half. Cook the beans and peas in boiling water for 2–3 minutes. Refresh under cold water and drain.

2 Cook the eggs in simmering water for 9 minutes, until the yolk is just set. Rinse under cold water. Peel and slice them into quarters.

3 If you are using fresh tuna, preheat the grill to moderate. Cut the tuna into slices 1cm (½in) thick, brush with olive oil, and grill for 2 minutes on each side, until just cooked. Remove from grill and flake. If using canned tuna, drain well then flake.

4 Arrange all the ingredients in a large bowl. Just before eating, pour over the Vinaigrette, toss, and serve with plenty of freshly sliced baguette.

COOK'S TIP
It is best to cut the eggs and add them to the salad just before serving.

QUINCE TART TATIN

⏱ 10 MINUTES 🍲 1 HOUR 55 MINUTES

INGREDIENTS

125G (4OZ) UNSALTED BUTTER
125G (4OZ) CASTER SUGAR
1KG (2LB) QUINCES, PEELED OR
PEARS, UNPEELED
3 TBSP BRANDY (OPTIONAL)
300G (10OZ) SWEET SHORTCRUST PASTRY,
CHILLED (SEE PAGE 184)
500ML (17FL OZ) WHIPPING CREAM
1 TBSP ICING SUGAR, SIFTED
2 TBSP BRANDY OR OTHER LIQUEUR

COOK'S TIP
If you are using the pastry recipe on page 184 make one and a half times the quantities given, or double the recipe and deep freeze the excess.

1 Heat the butter and sugar in a 23cm (9in) all-metal frying pan over a moderate heat until the mixture begins to caramelize. Remove from the heat.

2 Cut the quinces into quarters, remove the cores, then cut each quarter into 3 slices (if using pears, cut into quarters).

3 Arrange the fruit, core side up, in a radiating pattern in the pan. Cook over a low heat for 1 hour 30 minutes (40 minutes for pears), until soft, shaking the pan occasionally. Heat the brandy in a small pan or ladle, then set it alight and pour it over the fruit.

4 Preheat oven to 190°C/375°F/Gas 5. Roll out the pastry into a circle just a little larger than the pan. Lay it over the pan, tucking the edges down into the pan to cover the fruit. Bake for 20 minutes, until pale golden. Remove and cool for 5–10 minutes.

5 Meanwhile, make the brandied cream. Place the cream, icing sugar, and brandy in a large mixing bowl and whisk until the mixture forms soft peaks. Turn the tart tatin out onto a flat serving platter: the pastry now forms the base, the fruit the top. Serve with the brandied cream.

EXOTIC SPREAD FOR 12

SPICY CHICKEN WITH PAPAYA SALAD

🥄 35 MINUTES 🍲 50 MINUTES ▭ 2 HOURS SOAKING

INGREDIENTS

7CM (3IN) PIECE OF FRESH GINGER,
PEELED & COARSELY CHOPPED
4 GARLIC CLOVES, PEELED
2 FRESH RED CHILLIES, DESEEDED &
COARSELY CHOPPED
200ML (7FL OZ) COCONUT MILK
4 TBSP OLIVE OIL
24 CHICKEN THIGHS, BONED, SKINS ON
2 TBSP GROUND CORIANDER
3 TBSP GROUND CUMIN
3 TBSP CARDAMOMS, SEEDS CRUSHED
175G (6OZ) FRESH COCONUT, GRATED
& LIGHTLY TOASTED
3 LIMES, JUICE & GRATED ZEST
2 TBSP CASTER SUGAR
300ML (½ PT) WATER
5 TBSP FRESH
CORIANDER,
COARSELY
CHOPPED
150ML (¼ PT)
SHARP SWEET
DRESSING (SEE
PAGE 185)
4 LARGE RIPE
PAPAYA, PEELED
& THINLY
SLICED
6 COURGETTES,
CUT INTO THIN
STRIPS
1 CUCUMBER,
THINLY SLICED

1 In a blender, liquidize the ginger, garlic, chillies, and coconut milk to make a smooth paste.

2 Heat the oil in a large frying pan and cook the chicken in batches for approximately 5 minutes each side, until evenly browned. Remove from the pan and set aside.

3 To the pan, add the ground coriander, cumin, and cardamom seeds and cook over a high heat for about 2 minutes. Stir in the spice paste and cook for a further 2 minutes. Add the chicken, coconut, lime juice and zest, sugar, and water. Bring to the boil, cover, and simmer gently for 25 minutes. Add 2 tablespoons of the fresh coriander and leave to cool.

4 To make the salad, pour the Sharp Sweet Dressing over the slices of papaya, courgettes, and cucumber and leave to soak for at least 2 hours. Add the rest of the fresh coriander and serve with the chicken.

COOK'S TIPS

The chicken is also delicious served warm with the salad. If you wish, use mangoes instead of papaya.

SPICY CHICKEN WITH
PAPAYA SALAD

SPICY LAMB KEBABS

☑ 20 MINUTES ☐ 12 MINUTES ☐ 2 HOURS MARINATING

INGREDIENTS

3 TBSP SESAME OIL
2 TBSP GROUND CUMIN
2 TBSP OYSTER SAUCE
3 TBSP SHERRY VINEGAR
2 TBSP LIGHT SOY SAUCE
3 TBSP DRY SHERRY
3 GARLIC CLOVES, CRUSHED
6 MILD FRESH GREEN CHILLIES (PREFERABLY POBLANO OR ANCHO), FINELY CHOPPED
2 TBSP GROUND CUMIN
1 TBSP CLEAR HONEY
1.5KG (3LB) BONED LEG OF LAMB, CUBED
2 KIWI FRUITS, JUICE & PULP
24 METAL SKEWERS, OR WOODEN SKEWERS SOAKED FOR 1 HOUR

1 To make the marinade, heat the oil in a frying pan. Add the cumin and lightly brown for about 2 minutes. Stir in all the remaining ingredients (except the lamb and kiwi fruit), bring to the boil, then simmer for 5 minutes. Allow to cool.

2 Place the lamb in a large, non-metallic bowl and squeeze over the kiwi juice and pulp. Add the marinade. Cover, and leave to marinate in the refrigerator for 2–8 hours, turning the meat occasionally.

3 Preheat the grill to high. Line the base of the grill pan with foil.

4 Remove the lamb from the bowl, reserving the marinade. Thread the meat onto the skewers.

5 Baste the lamb with the marinade and cook for about 6 minutes per side, until crisp on the outside and just pink at the centre. Allow to cool.

COOK'S TIP
These kebabs may be prepared up to 3 days in advance and stored in the refrigerator.

INDIAN MILK PUDDING

☑ 10 MINUTES ☐ 25 MINUTES ☐ 12 HOURS CHILLING

INGREDIENTS

1.5 LITRES (2½ PT) MILK
500G (1LB) RISOTTO RICE
850ML (1½ PT) DOUBLE CREAM
1 TSP GROUND SAFFRON
12 CARDAMOMS, SEEDS CRUSHED
1 TBSP GROUND CORIANDER
3 BAY LEAVES
400G (13OZ) CASTER SUGAR
3 EGGS, LIGHTLY BEATEN
3 TSP VANILLA EXTRACT
1 TSP GROUND NUTMEG
CRÈME FRAÎCHE TO SERVE

1 In a large, heavy-based saucepan, heat the milk, rice, cream, saffron, cardamom seeds, coriander, bay leaves, and half of the sugar. Bring to the boil, then simmer, covered, for about 20 minutes, until the rice is *al dente*. Remove from the heat.

2 Discard the bay leaves. Beat in the eggs and vanilla until the mixture thickens. Pour into 2 rectangular 23 x 13cm (9 x 5in) loaf tins and leave to cool completely in a refrigerator, preferably overnight.

3 Turn the grill to high. Sprinkle the remaining sugar mixed with the nutmeg over the tops of the desserts, and grill as close to the heat as possible for about 2–5 minutes, until the sugar caramelizes. When cold, cut into slices and serve with crème fraîche.

COOK'S TIPS
Always grill the sugar topping as close to eating as possible. This pudding is also delicious served warm: after it has set overnight, heat it through gently in a moderate oven for about 15 minutes, before grilling the topping.

DINE IN STYLE FOR 6

DUCK & ROCKET SALAD

☑ 10 MINUTES ☐ 15 MINUTES ☐ 4 HOURS MARINATING

INGREDIENTS
4 DUCK BREASTS, SKINS LEFT ON
5 SPRIGS FRESH ROSEMARY
5 GARLIC CLOVES, SKINS LEFT ON, CRUSHED
UNDER THE FLAT OF A KNIFE
150ML (¼ PT) SHERRY VINEGAR OR
RED WINE VINEGAR
4 TBSP OLIVE OIL
SALT & PEPPER TO TASTE
24 BLACK OLIVES, PITTED & HALVED
ROCKET LEAVES TO SERVE
PARMESAN CHEESE, THINLY SLICED, TO GARNISH
VINAIGRETTE (SEE PAGE 185)

COOK'S TIP
Use sherry vinegar instead of
white wine vinegar when you
make the Vinaigrette.

1 Flatten the duck breasts to 5cm (2in) thick. Make diagonal slits in the skin, and prick all over with a fork. Place the rosemary and garlic over the base of a non-metallic dish and lay the duck in a single layer on top.

2 Combine the vinegar, 3 tablespoons of oil, and seasoning, and pour over the duck. Leave to marinate, covered, in the refrigerator for 4 hours; turn once.

3 Remove the duck and reserve the marinade. Heat the remaining oil in a large frying pan and brown the duck on both sides. Add the marinade, with the garlic and rosemary, and the olives. Cook over a moderate heat for a further 5 minutes on each side.

4 When the duck is cool enough to handle, remove the breasts and olives and wrap in clingfilm to keep them moist. When completely cool, remove the clingfilm.

5 Cut the duck into slices, 1cm (½ in) thick. Serve with the olives on a bed of rocket and garnish with Parmesan. Pour over the Vinaigrette.

DUCK & ROCKET
SALAD

FENNEL & CHEESE TART

 25 MINUTES   50 MINUTES

INGREDIENTS

375G (12OZ) SHORTCRUST PASTRY (SEE
PAGE 184)
4 EGGS: 1 YOLK ONLY, 3 WHOLE
30G (1OZ) BUTTER
1 TBSP VEGETABLE OIL
2 ONIONS, FINELY CHOPPED
1 GARLIC CLOVE, SKIN LEFT ON, CRUSHED
UNDER THE FLAT OF A KNIFE
2 FENNEL BULBS, CHOPPED
2 TSP FRESH THYME, FINELY CHOPPED
450ML (¾ PT) LIVE NATURAL YOGURT
SALT TO TASTE
PINCH OF GROUND NUTMEG
125G (4OZ) GRUYÈRE CHEESE, GRATED
100G (3½ OZ) WALNUTS, COARSELY CHOPPED,
PLUS WALNUT HALVES TO GARNISH
WALNUT DRESSING (SEE PAGE 185) TO SERVE

1 For the crust, roll out the pastry and press into a 25cm (10in) loose-bottomed, fluted tart tin. Prick the bottom of the pastry all over with a fork then refrigerate for 30 minutes.

2 Preheat oven to 190°C/375°F/Gas 5. Line the dough with greaseproof paper, fill with dried beans, and bake in the oven for 12 minutes. Remove the greaseproof paper and the beans. Brush the base of the tart with the egg yolk, and return it to the oven for a further 8 minutes.

3 To make the filling, heat the butter and oil in a pan and gently fry the onion, garlic, fennel, and thyme for 10 minutes, until soft. Discard the garlic.

4 In a large bowl, lightly beat the whole eggs, yogurt, salt, and nutmeg until just mixed. Stir in the Gruyère, chopped walnuts, and the onion and fennel mixture. Pour into the baked pastry case and top with halved walnuts.

5 Bake for 30 minutes, until the top is golden. Serve cold with a green leaf and walnut salad dressed with Walnut Dressing.

COOK'S TIPS

If you are using the pastry recipe on page 184 make one and a half times or double the quantities given and freeze the excess for up to six weeks. This tart will also make an excellent first course for a dinner or a delicious lunch.

POLENTA CAKE

 25 MINUTES   1 HOUR

INGREDIENTS

250G (8OZ) UNSALTED BUTTER, SOFTENED
200G (7OZ) CASTER SUGAR
3 EGGS
75G (2½ OZ) PINE NUTS, LIGHTLY TOASTED
100G (3½ OZ) RAISINS (PREFERABLY MUSCAT)
3 LEMONS: JUICE OF ½, GRATED ZEST OF 3
150G (5OZ) POLENTA
1 TSP BAKING POWDER
10 CARDAMOMS, SEEDS CRUSHED
WHIPPED CREAM OR CRÈME FRAÎCHE TO SERVE

1 Preheat oven to 160°C/325°F/Gas 3. Cream the butter and sugar until pale and fluffy, then add the eggs, one by one, beating between each addition.

2 Fold in the pine nuts, raisins, lemon juice and zest, then add the polenta, baking powder, and the cardamon seeds. Mix well.

3 Turn the mixture into a greased and floured 20cm (8in) springform cake tin and bake for 1 hour.

4 Leave the cake to cool in its tin for 10 minutes, then release the sides. Allow to stand for 20 minutes more, then transfer to a cake plate. Serve with a spoonful of whipped cream or crème fraîche.

COOK'S TIP

Try serving this cake warm as a lunch or dinner dessert; serve it with 150ml (¼ pint) double cream, whipped with the juice of half a lemon and 2 teaspoons of caster sugar.

AFTERNOON TEA & COFFEE MORNINGS

IN DAYS GONE BY, PEOPLE SEEMED TO HAVE THE TIME TO STOP FOR MORNING COFFEE OR AFTERNOON TEA. NOW, MOST OF US ARE TOO BUSY FOR MORE THAN A QUICK DRINK IN BETWEEN MAIN MEALS. SURELY IT IS TIME TO REVIVE THE CUSTOM, EVEN IF ONLY AT WEEKENDS, SO WITH FAMILY AND FRIENDS WE CAN ENJOY ONCE AGAIN THOSE DELICIOUS SCONES, MOIST CAKES, AND SANDWICHES.

Long-established teatime favourites like lemon sponge, shortbread, and buttered crumpets from the Traditional Tea menu (page 174) should be served on delicate china (right).

COTTAGE

"How long does getting thin

RECREATE CHILDHOOD MEMORIES with pastel-coloured floral china, feather-light cakes with pretty icing, a jug of flowers, and, of course, many cups of restorative tea.

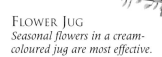

FLOWER JUG
Seasonal flowers in a cream-coloured jug are most effective.

CRYSTALLIZED PETALS

Decorate iced cakes with edible sugared rose petals to match your tableware. Arrange them to resemble flowers or just scatter on the cake.

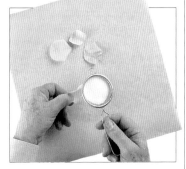

1 Carefully remove petals from rose flowerheads and paint both sides of each one with lightly beaten egg white.

2 Use a tea-strainer or small sieve to sprinkle both sides of each petal with caster sugar before the egg white dries.

CHOCOLATE LEAVES

Turn an iced cake into a feast for the eyes by decorating it with an extravagant bow and leaves made using your favourite kind of chocolate.

1 Melt chocolate until it is viscous but not runny. Paint it smoothly on one side of a firm, clean leaf.

2 Chill the chocolate until set, then gently peel the leaves off. Place among ribbons and bows as shown below.

FLORAL THEME
Arrange the sugared petals to resemble a flower. The green calyx is purely decorative and should not be eaten.

TRIMMINGS
Tie two lengths of silk ribbon in a sumptuous bow to make an enticing package.

take?' Pooh asked anxiously"
A.A. MILNE 1882–1956

CROCKERY
Evoke the mood of bygone days with fine floral china.

CAKE
Pink and yellow petals on a lemon sponge perpetuate a cottage garden theme.

LACE TABLECLOTH
Delicately flowered lace works very well with traditional china.

GARLANDS

Fresh linen festooned with flowers and

SWAGS OF SUMMER FLOWERS are perfect for occasions when we wish to impress, maybe at a garden party or christening tea.

FLORAL GARLAND

Make the garland by attaching bunches of wired flowers and leaves to lengths of light rope. Prepare small bunches of flowers and leaves first; you will need about 25 bunches per metre of garland. Allow yourself enough time: they cannot be hurried.

Fix to rope with turns of wire

1 Make a loop from which to hang the garland out of mossing wire, then securely tie this loop to the end of the rope.

2 Wire the first of your pre-prepared bunches of leaves and flowers to the rope so that it conceals the hanging loop.

NAPKIN FAN
Good for a crowd, paper napkins fanned out on a plate.

NEAT FINISH
If any wire shows, hide with foliage or cherries.

MIX & MATCH
*Smarten up the table
still further with a
silvery window box
filled with flowers to
match the garland.*

graceful china

TEA URN
*Combine practicality
with great elegance:
hire a decorative
tea urn for large
numbers of guests.*

*At least one stem must be
strong and 7cm (3in) long
to be wired onto rope*

*Twist wire round
full length of
stalks to secure*

3 Bring the reel of wire back
round, between the bunch
and the rope. This will stop the
bunch coming undone.

4 Bind the rope and stems
with wire. Add a second
bunch just behind the first, and
continue until the swag is filled.

LARGE BOW
*Use fine tacks to
hang the garland.
Adorn any joins
with a large bow.*

MENUS
"Stands the Church clock at ten to three?

TRADITIONAL TEA

Teatime favourites that are as wonderful served on the lawn in summer, as indoors in less clement weather. *Serves 12*

COFFEE, RUM & DATE CAKE
An exceedingly moist, syrup-soaked cake.

LEMON VICTORIA SPONGE
Simplicity itself: a light sponge redolent with piquant lemon.

CRUMPETS
Eat these warm, just with melting butter, with butter and honey, or with butter and fruit preserves.

BUTTERY SHORTBREAD
A Scottish speciality, these rich tasty biscuits are best when made at home.

DRINKS
Offer a choice of fragrant Orange Pekoe served without milk, or Earl Grey with or without milk.

PLANNING NOTES
Crumpets freeze particularly well, or they can be made up to one week ahead and kept in the refrigerator. Lightly toast to reheat, or serve straight from the griddle if cooking them once your guests have arrived. The cakes will keep in airtight tins for up to one week. *See pages 176–77 for recipes.*

FIRESIDE TEA

After a long afternoon walk, a heart-warming tea by a fire is more than a pleasure. *Serves 6*

SCONES
These are an English classic served warm with cream and jam, or just butter.

UPSIDE-DOWN CAKE
Once sampled, this could become a firm favourite.

MAIDS OF HONOUR
First made in the early eighteenth century in London, these curd tarts are justifiably still popular.

DRINKS
A choice of two teas: Lapsang Souchong served black, and a fine muscat-flavoured Darjeeling with milk if preferred.

PLANNING NOTES
The upside-down cake will keep for up to one week in an airtight tin. Scones are best eaten soon after baking and while still warm, although they can be stored in an airtight tin and then warmed through in the oven when required. They also freeze well. Maids of honour should be eaten the day they are made. *See pages 178–79 for recipes.*

"And is there honey still for tea?" RUPERT BROOKE 1887–1915

COFFEE AT ELEVEN

Advise your guests to have a small breakfast
and no lunch date when you invite them for
morning coffee! *Serves 6*

CHOCOLATE BROWNIES
*This American family recipe is rich in chocolate without
being too sweet and cloying.*

BANANA & WALNUT LOAF
*A sweet banana bread that is popular with both adults
and children.*

SPICY APPLE CAKE
*The topping of this moist, open-textured cake flavoured with
apple and spices is crunchy with sugar and nuts.*

DRINKS
*Jamaican Blue Mountain coffee made in a cafetiere
is the ideal choice for a special occasion.*

PLANNING NOTES
The banana and walnut loaf is good fresh, but delicious when
slightly stale (after a day) and lightly toasted. The brownies
and apple cake – best when fresh – can both be frozen, but
should then be eaten as soon as they have defrosted.
See pages 180–81 for recipes.

GARDEN PARTY TEA

An adaptable tea for large numbers on a special
occasion, perhaps at a Christening. *Serves 12*

BRANDY SNAPS
*Crisp ginger and brandy biscuits filled with
generous pipings of cream.*

NUTTY CHOCOLATE COOKIES
*No-flour cookies that are wickedly chocolatey, yet light
as a feather.*

FRUIT CAKE
*First boiled, then baked, this moist and fruity
cake is not too heavy.*

DRINKS
*Earl Grey tea, with or without milk, and a home-made
fruit drink such as Apple Punch (see page 137 for recipe)
for children.*

PLANNING NOTES
Decorate the fruit cake with whole almonds, or cover in
marzipan and ice for a special occasion. Un-iced it lasts for
two weeks in an airtight tin. Store the cookies in tins, too, for
a maximum of one week. Brandy snaps keep well for a few
days in an airtight tin. The cream can be piped in up to two
hours before tea. *See pages 182–83 for recipes.*

TRADITIONAL TEA FOR 12

COFFEE, RUM & DATE CAKE

 20 MINUTES 40 MINUTES 1 HOUR SOAKING

INGREDIENTS

200ML (7FL OZ) BOILING WATER
250G (8OZ) DRIED DATES, STONED &
COARSELY CHOPPED
2½ TBSP INSTANT COFFEE GRANULES
1 TSP BICARBONATE OF SODA
300G (10OZ) CASTER SUGAR
100G (3½OZ) UNSALTED BUTTER, SOFTENED
4 LARGE EGGS: 2 WHOLE, 2 WHITE ONLY
175ML (6OZ) PLAIN FLOUR, SIFTED
2 TSP BAKING POWDER, SIFTED
PINCH OF SALT
2 TSP VANILLA EXTRACT
3 TBSP DARK RUM
1KG (2LB) ICING SUGAR
2 TBSP LIQUID GLUCOSE OR CORN SYRUP

COOK'S TIP

Dust the cake with icing sugar at the end of step 4 for an equally delicious, and faster, alternative.

1 Pour half of the boiling water over the dates. Stir in the coffee and bicarbonate of soda. Leave to soak for 1 hour, then blend in a food processor.

2 Preheat oven to 180°C/350°F/Gas 4. Line a 20cm (8in) square or 23cm (9in) round cake tin with baking parchment then grease it and lightly dust with flour. Cream together 100g (3½oz) of caster sugar and 75g (2½oz) of butter until pale and fluffy. Lightly beat and add 2 whole eggs. Fold in the flour, baking powder, salt, and date mixture. Turn it into the tin and bake for 40 minutes.

3 To make the syrup, heat the vanilla and remaining water, caster sugar, and butter in a small saucepan and bring to the boil. Simmer for 15 minutes, then stir in the rum.

4 Leave the cake in its tin and pierce it all over with a skewer. Gradually pour over the syrup until it is absorbed into the cake. Cover the tin and leave overnight before turning out.

5 To make the roll-out icing, place the icing sugar in a large mixing bowl and gradually mix in the 2 egg whites and glucose. Knead for about 10 minutes, adding a little more icing sugar if the mixture is sticky. Roll out to fit the top and sides of the cake.

LEMON VICTORIA SPONGE

 25 MINUTES 30 MINUTES 1 HOUR SETTING

INGREDIENTS

250G (8OZ) SELF-RAISING FLOUR, SIFTED
2 TSP BAKING POWDER, SIFTED
375G (12OZ) UNSALTED BUTTER, SOFTENED
250G (8OZ) CASTER SUGAR
4 LARGE EGGS
1½ LEMONS, JUICE & GRATED ZEST
500G (1LB) ICING SUGAR, SIFTED
2 TBSP BOILING WATER
4 TBSP LEMON MARMALADE
CRYSTALLIZED PETALS (SEE PAGE 170)
TO DECORATE

1 Preheat oven to 180°C/350°F/Gas 4. In a large mixing bowl, combine the flour, baking powder, 250g (8oz) of the butter, the caster sugar, eggs, and lemon zest. Beat until well mixed.

2 Divide the mixture between two greased and lined 20cm (8in) loose-bottomed, round cake tins. Bake for about 30 minutes, until golden. Allow the cakes to cool for 2–3 minutes in their tins, then transfer to a wire rack to cool completely.

3 To make the icing, melt the remaining butter in a saucepan, remove from the heat, and beat in the icing sugar, boiling water, and finally the lemon juice.

4 Sandwich the cakes together with lemon marmalade. Spread half of the icing over the top and sides of the cake. Leave to set for 1 hour. Beat the remaining icing and spread it in soft swirls over the top and sides. Decorate with Crystallized Petals.

CRUMPETS

☑ 30 MINUTES   🍲 40 MINUTES
▢ 2 HOURS 30 MINUTES STANDING

INGREDIENTS
200ML (7FL OZ) MILK
1 TSP CASTER SUGAR
2 TSP EASY-BLEND YEAST
2 TBSP VEGETABLE OIL
550ML (18FL OZ) TEPID WATER
250G (8OZ) STRONG WHITE BREAD FLOUR
250G (8OZ) PLAIN FLOUR
2 TSP SALT
1 TSP BICARBONATE OF SODA

CRUMPETS

1 In a saucepan, heat the milk and sugar until the sugar has dissolved. Remove the pan from the heat and allow to cool slightly. Add the yeast, leave to stand for 10 minutes, then add the oil and 400ml (13fl oz) tepid water.

2 Sift both types of flour and salt into a mixing bowl. Gradually stir in the yeast mixture. Beat vigorously until smooth and elastic in consistency.

3 Cover the bowl with clingfilm and a tea towel leave in a warm place for 1½–2 hours until the mixture rises and the surface is full of bubbles.

4 Dissolve the bicarbonate of soda in the remaining water. Stir the batter so it collapses, add the bicarbonate of soda mixture, cover, and leave for a further 30 minutes.

5 Grease and flour three to five 8.5cm (3½in) plain ring moulds. Place on a griddle or frying pan over a gentle heat. Three-quarters fill each ring with batter and cook for 8 minutes, until the surface sets and bubbles. Turn (still in moulds) and cook for 4 minutes, until golden.

6 Push the crumpets out of the rings onto a tea towel laid over a wire rack. Cover with another tea towel and keep warm in a low oven. Re-grease the rings and cook the remaining batter. Serve warm with butter and honey or preserves.

BUTTERY SHORTBREAD

☑ 10 MINUTES   🍲 40 MINUTES

INGREDIENTS
220G (7OZ) PLAIN FLOUR
90G (3OZ) RICE FLOUR
½ TSP SALT
90G (3OZ) CASTER SUGAR
220G (7OZ) UNSALTED BUTTER, IN PIECES
45G (1½OZ) HAZELNUTS, COARSELY CHOPPED &
LIGHTLY TOASTED
ICING SUGAR TO DUST

1 Preheat oven to 160°C/325°F/Gas 3. Sift both types of flour and salt into a mixing bowl. Stir in the caster sugar.

2 Add the butter to the sifted ingredients. Using your fingertips, rub the butter into the flour until well blended. Add the hazelnuts, then knead the dough gently. Press the dough into a greased 23cm (9in) shallow square cake tin. Using a knife, indent halfway through the dough to mark into 24 fingers. Prick lightly with a fork.

3 Bake for about 40 minutes, until pale golden. Leave in the tin to cool. Cut into slices. Dust with icing sugar before serving.

FIRESIDE TEA FOR 6

SCONES

☑ 15 MINUTES 🍳 12 MINUTES

INGREDIENTS
250G (8OZ) PLAIN FLOUR
1 TBSP BAKING POWDER
45G (1½ OZ) CASTER SUGAR
90G (3OZ) BUTTER, IN PIECES
60G (2OZ) DRIED APRICOTS, COARSELY
CHOPPED, OR SULTANAS
1 LARGE EGG
90ML (3FL OZ) MILK
PRESERVES & CLOTTED CREAM TO SERVE

1 Preheat oven to 220°C/425°F/Gas 7. Sift the flour, baking powder, and sugar into a large bowl. Add the butter and, using your fingertips, rub it in until the mixture is the consistency of fine breadcrumbs. Stir in the apricots.

2 Beat together the egg and milk. Add gradually to the flour and butter mixture, reserving 2 tablespoons for glazing, until you have a soft dough that just comes away from the sides of the bowl.

3 Roll out the dough on a floured surface to about 2cm (¾ in) thick.

4 Cut out the dough using a 5cm (2in) round cutter. Place the scones on greased baking sheets and brush the tops with the reserved liquid. Bake for 10–12 minutes, until golden, then transfer to a wire rack.

5 Serve still slightly warm, halved, spread with apricot or other fruit preserve, and topped with fresh clotted cream or mascarpone cheese.

COOK'S TIP
Scones can be deep frozen for up to 6 weeks then defrosted and warmed in the oven.

UPSIDE-DOWN CAKE

☑ 20 MINUTES 🍳 55 MINUTES

INGREDIENTS
185G (6OZ) BUTTER, SOFTENED
185G (6OZ) SOFT BROWN SUGAR
½ LIME, GRATED ZEST & 1 TBSP JUICE
5 TBSP RUM (OPTIONAL)
7 RINGS OF FRESH OR CANNED PINEAPPLE
125G (4OZ) RAISINS
2 LARGE EGGS, LIGHTLY BEATEN
200G (7OZ) SELF-RAISING FLOUR
1 TSP BAKING POWDER
2 TBSP MILK

1 Preheat oven to 180°C/350°F/Gas 4. To make the topping, melt 60g (2oz) of the butter with 60g (2oz) of sugar and the lime juice in a small saucepan. Add 3 tablespoons of rum, if using. Pour the mixture into a greased 20cm (8in) round cake tin. Overlap the pineapple rings in the bottom of the tin and fill their centres and any gaps at the edges with half of the raisins.

2 To make the cake, combine the remaining ingredients (except for the raisins) in a large bowl and beat for 2 minutes.

3 Fold in the remaining raisins. Spread the cake mixture over the pineapple slices and smooth the surface flat.

4 Bake for about 50 minutes, until risen and golden. Leave in its tin for 5 minutes, then turn out onto a wire rack to cool.

COOK'S TIPS
If you are omitting the rum, add an extra tablespoon of lime juice to the topping and 1–2 tablespoons of milk to the cake mixture. If you use fresh pineapple, cut it into 1cm (½in) slices.

MAIDS OF HONOUR

15 MINUTES · 30 MINUTES · 30 MINUTES CHILLING

INGREDIENTS

175G (6OZ) PUFF PASTRY (SEE PAGE 184)
200ML (7OZ) CRÈME FRAÎCHE
1 EGG, LIGHTLY BEATEN
15G (½OZ) UNSALTED BUTTER, MELTED
1 TBSP CASTER SUGAR
½ LEMON, ZEST ONLY
½ TSP GROUND NUTMEG

1 Roll out the pastry. Using a 7.5cm (3in) cutter, cut out 12 rounds and press these into 12 bun tins. Lightly prick the pastry bases with a fork then refrigerate for 30 minutes.

2 Preheat oven to 190°C/375°C/Gas 5. In a large bowl, mix together the remaining ingredients (except the nutmeg). Spoon the mixture into the chilled pastry cases then sprinkle each of the tops with nutmeg.

3 Bake for 25–30 minutes until golden. Leave for 2 minutes before turning on to a wire rack to cool.

COOK'S TIP

Make a tasty variation by adding half a teaspoon of ground cardamom seeds to the filling.

MAIDS OF
HONOUR

UPSIDE-DOWN
CAKE

179

COFFEE AT ELEVEN FOR 6

CHOCOLATE BROWNIES

🥄 15 MINUTES 🍳 45 MINUTES

INGREDIENTS

3 TBSP PLAIN FLOUR
1 TSP BAKING POWDER
PINCH OF SALT
2 TBSP COCOA POWDER
175G (6OZ) PLAIN DARK CHOCOLATE
75G (2½ OZ) UNSALTED BUTTER
3 LARGE EGGS
250G (8OZ) CASTER SUGAR
1 TSP VANILLA EXTRACT
125G (4OZ) PECAN NUTS, LIGHTLY
TOASTED & COARSELY CHOPPED
4 TBSP SOURED CREAM

1 Preheat oven to 180°C/350°F/Gas 4. Sift together the flour, baking powder, salt, and cocoa.

2 Break the chocolate into small pieces, then heat with the butter in a double boiler, a heatproof bowl over a saucepan of simmering water, or in a microwave, until just melted (do not overheat). Stir gently until smooth, but do not beat. Leave to cool slightly.

3 In a mixing bowl, beat the eggs, sugar, and vanilla until thick. Fold in the chocolate mixture, pecans, soured cream, and the sifted ingredients.

4 Turn the mixture into a lined 23cm (9in) square cake tin. Bake for about 45 minutes (the outside will be set, the centre will be slightly soft). Cool in the tin for 30 minutes, then turn out onto a wire rack. When completely cool, cut into 12 squares.

COOK'S TIP
Walnuts, hazelnuts, or almonds can be used instead of pecan nuts if you prefer.

BANANA & WALNUT LOAF

🥄 10–15 MINUTES 🍳 1 HOUR

INGREDIENTS

250G (8OZ) SELF-RAISING FLOUR
½ TSP BICARBONATE OF SODA
PINCH OF SALT
½ LIME, JUICE ONLY
250G (8OZ) BANANA, MASHED
90G (3OZ) UNSALTED BUTTER, SOFTENED
125G (4OZ) SUGAR
2 LARGE EGGS, LIGHTLY BEATEN
3 TBSP BUTTERMILK OR SMETANA
60G (2OZ) WALNUTS, COARSELY CHOPPED

1 Preheat oven to 180°C/350°F/Gas 4. Sift together the flour, bicarbonate of soda, and salt. Sprinkle the lime juice over the mashed banana.

2 In a large mixing bowl, cream together the butter and sugar until pale and fluffy, then add the beaten eggs and banana and lime. Finally, gently fold in the sifted ingredients alternately with the chopped walnuts and buttermilk, until all the ingredients are thoroughly combined.

3 Turn the mixture into a greased 23cm x 13cm (9in x 5in) loaf tin. Bake for 1 hour, until the loaf has risen and is golden. Leave in its tin for 5 minutes, then turn out onto a wire rack to cool. Serve with unsalted butter.

COOK'S TIP
You can substitute chopped pecans, hazelnuts, or almonds for the walnuts.

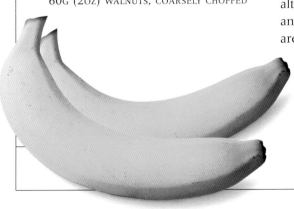

SPICY APPLE
CAKE

BANANA &
WALNUT LOAF

SPICY APPLE CAKE

20 MINUTES   55 MINUTES

INGREDIENTS
475G (15OZ) SUGAR
125G (4OZ) UNSALTED BUTTER, MELTED
100G (3½ OZ) PECAN NUTS, COARSELY CHOPPED
1 TSP GROUND CLOVES
625G (1¼ LB) GREEN COOKING APPLES
5 TBSP WATER
3 LARGE EGGS
2 TSP VANILLA EXTRACT
275G (9OZ) PLAIN FLOUR, SIFTED
2 TSP BAKING POWDER, SIFTED
1 TSP GROUND CINNAMON
PINCH OF SALT
75G (2½ OZ) DRIED APPLE OR DRIED PEAR,
COARSELY CHOPPED

1 Preheat oven to 190°C/375°F/Gas 5. First, prepare the topping. Combine 150g (5oz) of the sugar, 75g (2½oz) of the butter, the pecans, and ½ teaspoon of ground cloves. Set aside.

2 Next, make the apple purée: peel, core, and cut the cooking apples into chunks. Place in a saucepan with the water and cook, covered, for 8 minutes, until soft. Liquidize in a blender to make a purée.

3 In a large mixing bowl, beat the eggs and vanilla until thickened, then add the remaining sugar. Fold in the flour, baking powder, cinnamon, salt, and remaining cloves, then the apple purée, remaining butter, and dried apple.

4 Turn the mixture into a lined and greased 23cm (9in) springform cake tin. Bake for 15 minutes, then remove from the oven and spoon over the topping. Return the cake to the oven and bake for a further 25–30 minutes. Leave in its tin until completely cool.

COOK'S TIP
If time is short, use 250ml (8oz) shop-bought apple sauce instead of making the purée (step 2).

GARDEN PARTY TEA FOR 12

BRANDY SNAPS

10 MINUTES 16 MINUTES

INGREDIENTS
60G (2OZ) UNSALTED BUTTER
4 TBSP CASTER SUGAR
4 TBSP GOLDEN SYRUP
1 TBSP BRANDY (OPTIONAL)
4 TBSP PLAIN FLOUR, SIFTED
1 TSP GROUND GINGER
BRANDIED CREAM (SEE PAGE 163, STEP 5)

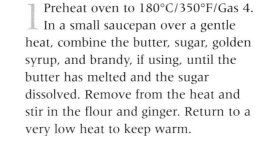

1 Preheat oven to 180°C/350°F/Gas 4. In a small saucepan over a gentle heat, combine the butter, sugar, golden syrup, and brandy, if using, until the butter has melted and the sugar dissolved. Remove from the heat and stir in the flour and ginger. Return to a very low heat to keep warm.

2 Line 2 baking sheets with baking parchment. Drop 3 teaspoons of mixture onto each sheet, about 12cm (5in) apart, spreading in a circular motion to make 10cm (4in) rounds.

3 Bake for 7–8 minutes, until golden. Leave to cool for 1 minute, then roll each biscuit around the oiled handle of a wooden spoon. If the biscuits become too hard to roll, return to the oven briefly to soften. Remove and place on a wire rack to cool. Continue to bake and roll batches of biscuits until all the mixture is used.

4 Prepare the Brandied Cream. Pipe the cream into each end of the brandy snap cylinders.

COOK'S TIP
This mixture will also make six Ginger Baskets. Bake six large biscuits in the same way then drape each one over an upturned teacup to form a fluted bowl. When cold, remove the cup.

NUTTY CHOCOLATE COOKIES

25 MINUTES 10 MINUTES

INGREDIENTS
200G (7OZ) PLAIN DARK CHOCOLATE
4 LARGE EGGS, WHITES ONLY
200G (7OZ) CASTER SUGAR
2 TSP VANILLA EXTRACT
1 TSP WHITE WINE VINEGAR
200G (7OZ) PECAN NUTS, COARSELY CHOPPED
& LIGHTLY TOASTED

COOK'S TIPS
These cookies keep well for at least 1 week in an airtight container. Walnuts, almonds, or hazelnuts could be used instead of pecans.

1 Preheat oven to 190°C/375°F/Gas 5. Break the chocolate into small pieces, then heat in a double boiler, a heatproof bowl over a saucepan of simmering water, or in a microwave. Stir the chocolate gently as it melts, but do not beat. Allow to cool slightly.

2 In a large bowl, whisk the egg whites until they form soft peaks. Add the sugar, a little at a time, whisking after each addition, until the peaks hold firm.

3 Fold in the vanilla and vinegar, then the melted chocolate and pecans.

4 Line 2 baking sheets with baking parchment and drop 12 large tablespoons of mixture onto each sheet, about 7cm (3in) apart, slightly smoothing down the mixture to make 6cm (2½in) discs.

5 Bake for 10 minutes (they should be slightly sticky). Leave on the baking sheet for 1 minute, then transfer to a wire rack to cool.

FRUIT CAKE

10 MINUTES · 1 HOUR 30 MINUTES · 2 HOURS COOLING

INGREDIENTS

125G (4OZ) UNSALTED BUTTER
175G (6OZ) SUGAR
375G (12OZ) RAISINS
250G (8OZ) SULTANAS
4 EARL GREY TEA BAGS
250ML (8FL OZ) WATER
2 LIMES, JUICE & GRATED ZEST
1 TSP BICARBONATE OF SODA
125G (4OZ) PLAIN FLOUR
125G (4OZ) SELF-RAISING FLOUR
1 TSP GROUND CLOVES
1 TSP GROUND NUTMEG
PINCH OF SALT
2 LARGE EGGS, LIGHTLY BEATEN
60G (2OZ) WHOLE ALMONDS

1 In a saucepan, heat the butter, sugar, raisins, sultanas, tea bags, water, lime juice and zest, and bicarbonate of soda. Bring to the boil, then simmer for 5 minutes. Squeeze the tea bags gently into the liquid to release their flavour.

2 Leave the mixture to cool for about 2 hours. Discard the tea bags.

3 Preheat oven to 180°C/350°F/Gas 4. In a large mixing bowl, sift together both types of flour, the cloves, nutmeg, and salt. Add the eggs and then the fruit mixture. Mix well.

4 Line and grease a 20cm (8in) round cake tin. Spoon in the cake mixture. Arrange the almonds over the top of the cake.

5 Bake for about 1¼–1½ hours, until golden. Leave the cake in its tin for 10 minutes, then transfer to a wire rack to cool.

COOK'S TIP

This cake will keep extremely well in an airtight tin for up to 3 weeks.

NUTTY
CHOCOLATE
COOKIES

FRUIT CAKE

BASIC RECIPES

PASTRY

PUFF PASTRY

INGREDIENTS FOR 750G (1½LB)
375G (12OZ) PLAIN FLOUR, SIFTED
PINCH OF SALT
375G (12OZ) BUTTER, WELL CHILLED,
IN PIECES
10 TBSP ICE COLD WATER
3 TSP LEMON JUICE

Place the flour, salt, and butter in a large mixing bowl. Using a knife, toss the butter pieces in the flour until they are well coated. Mix the water with the lemon juice and add to the bowl, using the knife to mix in the liquid and keeping the butter in pieces as long as possible.

When the mix just binds together turn onto a floured surface and roll into a rectangle about 15 x 35cm (6 x 14in). Fold the top third of the rectangle down then the bottom third up over it. Press the edges together to seal. Wrap in a plastic bag or clingfilm and refrigerate for 15 minutes. Remove from the refrigerator, place on a floured surface, and with the unfolded edges at the top and bottom, roll into a rectangle, fold and seal as before, and refrigerate for 15 minutes.

Repeat this process twice more, then refrigerate for 30 minutes before using.

SHORTCRUST PASTRY

INGREDIENTS FOR 500G (1LB)
300G (10OZ) PLAIN FLOUR, SIFTED
PINCH OF SALT
75G (2½OZ) BUTTER, IN PIECES
75G (2½OZ) LARD OR VEGETABLE FAT,
IN PIECES
2 TSP ICE COLD WATER

Place the flour, salt, butter, and lard in a food processor and work until the mixture is the consistency of breadcrumbs.

Add the water and process until the mix just holds together, adding a little more water if necessary.

Gather the mixture into a soft ball and wrap in a plastic bag or clingfilm. Refrigerate for at least 30 minutes before using.

SWEET SHORTCRUST PASTRY

INGREDIENTS FOR 500G (1LB)
250G (8OZ) PLAIN FLOUR, SIFTED
PINCH OF SALT
60G (2OZ) CASTER SUGAR
150G (5OZ) UNSALTED BUTTER, IN PIECES
2 LARGE EGGS, YOLKS ONLY, LIGHTLY BEATEN

Place the flour, salt, sugar, and butter in a food processor and work until the mixture is the consistency of breadcrumbs.

Add the egg yolks and process briefly until the mix just binds together.

Wrap in a plastic bag or clingfilm and refrigerate for 1 hour before using.

COOK'S PASTRY TIPS

When making pastry without a food processor, cut the butter into the dry ingredients using a knife, or mix them together with your fingertips. When the mixture is the consistency of breadcrumbs, gradually cut in or mix in the egg yolks.

Use chilled water to make pastry dough and add just enough to make the dough bind. It is important to add the liquid carefully as too much will make the cooked pastry tough and too little will produce a crumbly baked pastry.

If you have time, leave the pastry to rest in the refrigerator for more than 30 minutes: this helps to stop it shrinking when you bake it.

When baking blind, brush the base of the case with about 2 tablespoons lightly beaten egg yolk after removing the beans from the case, before returning the pastry to the oven: this prevents the case going soggy when the filling is added.

Pastry can be frozen for up to 6 weeks or kept in the refrigerator for 3 days.

STOCKS

FOR 3 LITRES (5PT)

VEGETABLE STOCK

3 TBSP OLIVE OIL
4 ONIONS, FINELY CHOPPED
4 CELERY STICKS, CHOPPED
4 CARROTS, CHOPPED
2 BAY LEAVES
1 TBSP FRESH OREGANO, FINELY CHOPPED
½ TSP GROUND GINGER
2 TSP SALT
3 LITRES (5PT) WATER

Heat the oil in a large saucepan, add the onions, celery, and carrots and cook over a moderate heat for 6 minutes. Add the remaining ingredients, bring to the boil, then simmer for 1 hour 30 minutes. Strain through a fine sieve and allow to cool. Refrigerate or freeze (for up to six weeks) until needed.

FISH STOCK

500G (1LB) RAW PRAWNS, SHELLS ON
8 ANCHOVY FILLETS
ANY OTHER FISH BONES & SKIN (OPTIONAL)
3 LITRES (5PT) WATER
3 ONIONS, FINELY CHOPPED
1 BAY LEAF
1 LEMON, JUICE ONLY
SALT TO TASTE

Crush the prawns in their shells and place them with all the remaining ingredients (except the salt) in a large saucepan. Bring to the boil then simmer, covered, for 1 hour 30 minutes, skimming occasionally to remove any scum. Remove from the heat and add salt to taste. Strain through a fine sieve and allow to cool. Refrigerate or freeze until needed.

CHICKEN STOCK

2 CHICKEN CARCASSES
3 LITRES (5PT) WATER
3 ONIONS, FINELY CHOPPED
2 TSP GROUND BLACK PEPPER
4 GARLIC CLOVES, CRUSHED
1 BAY LEAF
2 TSP FRESH THYME, FINELY CHOPPED

Place all the ingredients in a saucepan and bring to the boil. Simmer, covered, for 2 hours 30 minutes, skimming occasionally to remove any scum. Strain through a fine sieve and allow to cool. Refrigerate or freeze (for up to 6 weeks) until needed.

SALAD DRESSINGS

FOR 12 SERVINGS

WALNUT OR HAZELNUT

3 TSP WHITE WINE VINEGAR
4 TSP LEMON JUICE
PINCH SALT, PEPPER & SUGAR
4 TBSP WALNUT OR HAZELNUT OIL
6 TBSP VEGETABLE OIL

Whisk the vinegar and lemon juice with the salt, pepper, and sugar until well mixed. Drizzle in the oils slowly, beating all the time to form an emulsion. It will keep covered in the refrigerator for up to 1 week.

VINAIGRETTE

4 TSP WHITE WINE VINEGAR
4 TSP DIJON MUSTARD
PINCH SALT & PEPPER
10 TBSP OLIVE OIL

Whisk the vinegar, mustard, and seasoning until well mixed. Slowly drizzle in the olive oil, beating all the time until it forms a thick, creamy sauce. It will keep covered in the refrigerator for up to 1 week.

SHARP SWEET

3 LIMES, JUICE & GRATED ZEST
½ FRESH GREEN CHILLI
2 GARLIC CLOVES, CRUSHED
PINCH SALT & PEPPER
3 TBSP WATER
3 TSP SUGAR

Deseed and finely chop the chilli. Whisk all the ingredients together until well mixed. It will keep covered in the refrigerator for up to 1 week. This dressing is excellent served with salads including exotic fruits such as mango and papaya.

ACCOMPANIMENTS

FOR 12 SERVINGS

FOCACCIA

1 PACKET EASY BLEND YEAST
2 TSP SALT
1KG (2LB) STRONG WHITE BREAD FLOUR
8 TBSP OLIVE OIL
450ML (¾ PT) TEPID WATER
1 TBSP SEA SALT CRYSTALS
2 TBSP FRESH SAGE, FINELY CHOPPED

Mix the yeast, salt, 500g (1lb) of the flour, 3 tablespoons of the olive oil and about 200ml (7fl oz) of water in a large bowl. Gradually work in the remaining flour and as much water as it takes to make a soft but not sticky dough.

Knead the dough on a floured surface for 15 minutes until smooth and elastic. Place it in a large, oiled plastic bag and leave to rise at warm room temperature for 1½–2 hours.

Punch the risen dough down and form it into a flat rectangle about 1cm (½in) thick. Place it on a lightly oiled baking sheet, cover with plastic, and let it rise again for 45 minutes. Preheat oven to 230°C/450°F/Gas 8.

After the second rising, make dents with your fingertips all over the top of the dough and brush on a mix of the remaining olive oil whisked with 2 tablespoons of tepid water. This mix will run into the holes made by your fingers. Sprinkle with the sea salt and sage, and bake for 20–25 minutes.

NEW POTATO SALAD

1½KG (3LB) SMALL NEW POTATOES
1 TBSP RED WINE VINEGAR
2 TBSP WHOLEGRAIN MUSTARD
2 TBSP FRESH DILL, FINELY CHOPPED
SALT & PEPPER TO TASTE
7 TBSP OLIVE OIL
1 GARLIC CLOVE, HALVED

Cook the potatoes in a large saucepan of gently boiling salted water until just cooked, but not soft. The cooking time will depend on the variety of potato you use. Drain immediately, and as soon as you can handle the potatoes cut them into medium-thick slices.

In a small bowl, mix the vinegar, mustard, dill, and seasoning very well, then drizzle in the oil, beating all the time until you have a good emulsion. Rub a serving dish with the cut edges of the garlic, tip in the warm potatoes, and gently toss them in the dressing.

HERBY POTATOES

3 TBSP OLIVE OIL
1.5KG (3LB) NEW POTATOES, CUT INTO HALVES
4 GARLIC CLOVES, CRUSHED
2 TBSP EACH FRESH THYME & FRESH MARJORAM, FINELY CHOPPED
2 BAY LEAVES, TORN
SALT TO TASTE
VEGETABLE STOCK (SEE PAGE 185)

Heat the oil in a large saucepan, add the potatoes and garlic, and sauté until they just begin to brown. Add the thyme, marjoram, bay leaves, salt, and enough vegetable stock to come just over halfway up the potatoes. Boil gently, uncovered, for 30 minutes, until little water remains.

Remove from the heat and chop the potatoes, incorporating the remaining liquid in the saucepan, until they are the consistency of coarse mashed potato.

COOK'S TIPS
You may need to adjust the seasoning once you have chopped the potatoes. Halve the recipe to serve 6 people, or make 2 batches if you are catering for larger numbers.

BAY ROAST POTATOES

12 BAKING POTATOES, SCRUBBED
1 TBSP OLIVE OIL
1 TSP SALT
12 BAY LEAVES, CUT IN HALF WIDTHWISE

Preheat oven to 200°C/400°F/Gas 6. Make two deep cuts into each potato, about three-quarters of the way through. Rub each potato with oil then slip the half bay leaves into the cuts.

Place on a baking sheet, sprinkle salt onto the potatoes, and bake for about 1 hour, or until brown and cooked through (the cooking time may vary depending on the size of the potatoes, so test them with a skewer).

COOK'S TIP
Good red-skinned potatoes are excellent when cooked this way.

ROAST SHALLOTS

36 SHALLOTS, PEELED
60G (2OZ) BUTTER
2 TSP SUGAR

Place the shallots, butter, and sugar in a heavy frying pan (with a lid). Cook over a moderate heat, shaking occasionally until the shallots begin to colour. Turn the heat down to the lowest setting and cook, covered, for 30 minutes, until the shallots are nutty brown and cooked through.

BRAISED CHICORY

125G (4OZ) BUTTER
12 HEADS OF CHICORY, HALVED
2 LEMONS, JUICE & GRATED ZEST

Preheat oven to 180°C/375°F/Gas 5. Heat the butter in a frying pan, add the chicory, and lightly brown all over. Remove from the heat and arrange in a single layer in a shallow baking dish with a lid, using two dishes if necessary. Pour over the lemon juice and sprinkle with the zest.

Cover the dish and bake for 1 hour, remove lid, and continue to cook for 20 minutes, or until chicory is brown and caramelized. Serve two halves each.

CELERIAC RÉMOULADE

650G (1LB 6OZ) CELERIAC, PEELED
1 LEMON, JUICE & GRATED ZEST
6 TBSP MAYONNAISE (SEE PAGE 147)
3 TBSP DIJON MUSTARD
¼ TSP GROUND CHILLI POWDER
SALT TO TASTE

Coarsely grate the celeriac then toss immediately in the lemon juice. Add the remaining ingredients and stir briskly to ensure that the celeriac is well coated.

COOK'S TIP
This recipe is also delicious made with half celeriac, half grated fresh carrot. Double or halve the quantities proportionately.

COUSCOUS

2 TBSP SESAME OIL
4 TSP GROUND CORIANDER
4 TSP GROUND TURMERIC
1 LITRE (1¾ PT) WATER
125G (4OZ) SULTANAS
SALT TO TASTE
750G (1½LB) COUSCOUS
125G (4OZ) BUTTER

Heat the oil, coriander, and turmeric in a saucepan and cook until the spices begin to brown. Add the water, sultanas and salt, and bring to the boil.

Remove from the heat and add the couscous in a steady stream, stirring all the time. Cover, and leave to stand for 10 minutes. Add the butter, and cook over a low heat for 5 minutes, stirring continuously. It can be kept warm in a low oven for up to 2 hours, covered tightly. Fluff with a fork before serving.

SAFFRON RICE

750G (1½LB) BASMATI RICE
60G (2OZ) BUTTER
1 TBSP OLIVE OIL
3 GARLIC CLOVES, SKINS LEFT ON, CRUSHED
UNDER THE FLAT OF A KNIFE
660ML (22FL OZ) CHICKEN STOCK (SEE
PAGE 185) OR WATER
1 TSP SAFFRON THREADS, CRUSHED
3 TSP SALT

Wash the rice in a sieve under running water until the water runs clear.

Heat the butter, oil, and garlic in a large saucepan over a medium heat. When the butter has melted, add the rice and stir until well coated. Add the Chicken Stock, saffron, and salt, stir well, and bring to the boil. Turn the heat to low and cook, covered, for 8 minutes. Remove from the heat, discard the garlic, and allow to stand for 3 minutes with the lid on before serving.

RECIPE LIST

BREAKFASTS

Bubble & Squeak 42
Coeur à la Crème & Passion Fruit 40
Cranberry Muffins 37
Creamy Scrambled Eggs 43
Golden Corn & Green Pea Pancakes 39
Herbed Tomatoes 43
Mango & Papaya 36
Orange & Lime Marmalade 43
Pernod Pears in Grapefruit Juice 38
Prosciutto, Prawns & Apples 38
Provençal Pipérade 37
Rich Lemon Curd 41
Spicy Kedgeree 41

BREADS & CAKES

Banana & Walnut Loaf 180
Brandy Snaps 182
Buttery Shortbread 177
Chocolate Birthday Cake 115
Chocolate Brownies 180
Coffee, Rum & Date Cake 176
Crumpets 177
Focaccia 186
Fruit Cake 183
Home-baked Oat Biscuits 120
Lemon Victoria Sponge 176
Maids of Honour 179
Nutty Chocolate Cookies 182
Raisin & Oregano Soda Bread 160
Scones 178
Spicy Apple Cake 181
Upside-down Cake 178

STARTERS

Asparagus & Ham Fettucine 102
Brie & Lentil Salad 90
Crab Tartlets with Leek Purée 82
Duck & Rocket Salad 166
Fig & Feta Salad 54
Herb Omelette with Caviar 84

Italian Cabbage Soup 100
Marinated Salmon 118
Prawns in Cider 94
Prawn, Leek & Saffron Soup 98
Peppered Scallops 86
Rocket Soup 88
Roast Tomato Soup 92
Salad Niçoise 163
Seared Goat's Cheese & Tapenade 150
Seared Pears & Parma Ham 80
Tiger Prawn Soup 56
Potato & Bacon Salad 58
Wild Mushroom Ragoût 96

MAIN COURSES

Blue Cheese Soufflés 92
Broccoli & Pine Nut Fettucine 116
Charred Squid 146
Chicken Crêpe Gâteau 118
Crispy Chicken Livers 148
Cassoulet 114
Duck with Kumquats 83
Fennel & Cheese Tart 167
Fish Cakes with Herb Sauce 63
Flemish-style Beef 98
Fresh Pan-fried Sardines 54
Ginger & Garlic Chicken 152
Herbed Country Pâté 161
Lamb Tagine with Couscous 87
Lobster with Roast Figs 84
Mixed Mushroom Kebabs 151
Oriental Parcels with Spicy Sauce 57
Parslied Ham 161
Peppered Lamb 58
Pheasant & Apples with Calvados 97
Pissaladière 162
Pork with Tuna Sauce 121
Prawn & Mushroom Papardelle 116
Red Mullet with Fennel & Orange 147
Scallops with Chard 80
Seared Beef with Thai Sauce 153
Spicy Chicken with Papaya Salad 164

Spicy Lamb Kebabs 165
Spicy Pork Roast 100
Tarragon Chicken 88
Tea-smoked Tuna 148
Tuna Steaks with Rhubarb 94
Trout with Gooseberry Sauce 91
Vegetable & Nut Kebabs 102

DESSERTS

Aromatic Fruit Salad 55
Blueberry Tart 61
Chocolate & Coffee Cheesecake 97
Chocolate Tart 81
Coconut & Saffron Ice Cream 87
Coffee & Amaretto Ice Cream 117
Coffee Truffle Puddings 93
Fresh Fruit Savarin 119
Ginger Sorbet 57
Indian Milk Pudding 165
Lime & Mint Mould 89
Mango Syllabub & Almond Biscuits 95
Miraculous Blackberry Cake 101
Orange & Grapefruit Sorbets 85
Peppered Pineapple 147
Polenta Cake 167
Quince Tart Tatin 163
Roasted Plantains with Rum Sauce 149
Spiced Quinces & Earl Grey Sorbet 103
Steamed Cranberry Pudding 99
Strawberry Tart 91
Summer Fruits with Crème Fraîche 83
West Indian Punch Jelly 121
Winter Compote & Prune Ice Cream 59

COCKTAIL FOOD

Cocktail Kebabs 130
Crostini 132
Filo Parcels 131
Fruits with Parma Ham 131
Sushi 133

INDEX

ACKNOWLEDGMENTS

AUTHOR'S ACKNOWLEDGMENTS

Working on this book has been a joy. Firstly, I would like to thank photographers Martin Brigdale and Stephen Hayward for their magnificent photography: Martin for the food, and Stephen for the flowers and the table settings.

Thank you also to the wonderful DK team of editor Lesley (munch) Malkin and art editor Murdo (munch, munch) Culver.

Thanks, too, to Helen Trent, who, with her magic eye (and the odd few sneezes), located so much beautiful china, glass, cutlery, and table linen. Janey Suthering and Janice Murfitt did the most wonderful job of preparing all the food for the photographic sessions – eating the spoils at lunchtime was a very special bonus!

Dennis, Lee, and David at John Austin, New Covent Garden Market, were the usual, invaluable aids, especially at finding so many out-of-season flowers. My appreciation as well to Terracottas, also of New Covent Garden, for the loan of special containers. Finally, and most importantly, I would like to thank Rodney "Cocktails" Engen for all his constructive help with the book and also, together with a big heap of my friends, for being a guinea pig for a year while I was making and testing all the recipes.

PUBLISHER'S ACKNOWLEDGMENTS

Thank you to Anna Cheifetz and Polly Boyd for editorial help, particularly on the recipes, and also to Susie Behar and Richard Hammond. For additional design help, thanks to Pauline Clarke, Sharon Moore, and Deborah Myatt. We would also like to thank Emma Patmore for testing the recipes, with the exception of those in the Breakfast & Brunch, Lunch, and Afternoon Tea & Coffee Mornings chapters; thank you to Jill Eggleton, who tested these. Thanks also to Mark Bracey for DTP guidance, and to Hilary Bird for compiling the index.

PICTURE CREDITS

All food photography by Martin Brigdale, and all other photography by Stephen Hayward, with the exception of:

Alan Williams 29 tc; Dave King 41 tr, 60 bl, 91 br, 114 tr, 145 tl; David Murray 58 cl, 96 tr, 114 bl; Ian O'Leary 83 cl, 145 tc, 175 tc; Jacqui Hurst 77 tc; Joe Cornish 49 tr; John Glover 175 tr; Martin Norris 56 tr; Matthew Ward 79 tl; Max Alexander 145 tr; Philip Dowell 147 br, 153 br, 166 tr, 182 cl; Steven Wooster 71 tc, 77 tr, 79 tr, 159 tr, 171 tc.

t=top, c=centre, b=bottom, r=right, l=left

THE FOLLOWING KINDLY LOANED US PROPS FOR PHOTOGRAPHY

DIVERTIMENTI
44 Fulham Road
London SW3 6HH

For serving dishes, pasta bowls, and plates used on pages: 22–3, 27, 28–9, 139, and 140–41.

THOMAS GOODE & CO (LONDON) LTD
19 South Audley Street
London W1Y 6BN

For serving dishes, plates, cutlery, glasses, and place mats used on pages: 63, 64–5, 105, and 106–7.

VILLEROY & BOCH
267 Merton Road
London SW19 5JS

For glasses, cutlery, and plates used on pages: 110–11.